W9-BBA-159

What Were the Crusades?

What Were the Crusades?

JONATHAN RILEY-SMITH

Rowman and Littlefield
Totowa, New Jersey

First published in the United States 1977 by
ROWMAN AND LITTLEFIELD, Totowa, N.J.
Reprinted 1978

First published in the United Kingdom 1977 by
The Macmillan Press Ltd

Printed in Great Britain

Library of Congress Cataloging in Publication Data

Riley-Smith, Jonathan Simon Christopher, 1938–
    What were the Crusades?

    Bibliography: p.
    Includes index.
    1. Crusades. I. Title.
D157.R54 1977   909.07   76–54981
ISBN 0–87471–944–5

IN MEMORIAM
John James Craik Henderson, 1890–1971

Contents

Preface

In this book I have put down thoughts that have developed in over a decade of lecturing to and supervising students at the universities of St Andrews and Cambridge, so my first expression of thanks must be to them, especially Dr Bruce Beebe, whose unpublished thesis on King Edward I of England and the crusades is a good study of an aspect of the movement in the late thirteenth century. I am glad to have the chance of stating again how much I appreciate the wise advice of Dr R. C. Smail, my *magister,* who read the book in typescript, as did my wife, whose reactions as a 'general reader' have been of great value to me. I am, as always, grateful to her and to my children for providing the kind of environment in which I find it easy to work.

Cambridge   J. S. C. R.-S.

1 *What Were the Crusades?*

THE crusading movement was one of the great forces in our history. Fought on a vast scale, in terms of both geography and the numbers of men involved, the crusades dominated the thoughts and feelings of western Europeans between 1095 and 1400 so profoundly that there was scarcely a writer on contemporary affairs who did not at some point refer to one of them or to the fate of the states established in their wake on the eastern shores of the Mediterranean, in Spain and along the Baltic coast. They still had some appeal as late as the eighteenth century. Even today it is hard to be indifferent to their history: they were launched in support of a cause which can be portrayed with equal force as the most noble and the most ignoble, and over the centuries men have turned to them for inspiration or as an object lesson in human corruptibility. In modern times the French have seen them as the first of their nation's colonial enterprises; in Palestine the British in 1917 and the Israelis in the last few decades have felt themselves to be the inheritors of their traditions; and a movement in the modern Christian Churches, consisting of the theologians of Liberation and the activists of the new Left, expresses, without seeming to realise the fact, some of the ideas of the crusading apologists. For good or ill the crusades introduced new forces into the politics of the eastern Mediterranean region which were to last for over 600 years and they helped to foster elements in Latin Christianity which are now seen as integral to it.

Yet, after nearly a millenium of interest and centuries of academic study, very few people have any clear idea of what a crusade was. A recent historian, Professor H. E. Mayer, has drawn attention to the extraordinary way in which a great deal of research is going on into the subject without there being any commonly agreed starting-point and he has appealed for 'an unambiguous, lucid and generally accepted definition of the term "crusade" '. In writing this little book I have had the modest aim of defining it as simply as possible and of at least stimulating some discussion of first principles. I hope it will prove useful as something to which students can turn before they read the more ambitious histories.

Definition is by no means easy. One cannot help wondering how to avoid gross over-simplification when trying to describe something which dominated Europe for so long. There are, moreover, very few clear descriptions to be found in medieval writings and it has been suggested recently that the fragmentary treatment given to the subject by canon lawyers and theologians is evidence for their reluctance to link the Church too positively to violence: it has never been easy for Christian writers to reconcile Christ's statements on force with the apparent necessity for order and stability in this world. There was no one term consistently used to describe the crusade or its participants. Besides the various vernacular words that appeared in the thirteenth century, like *croiserie* in French and English, it could be called a pilgrimage (*iter* or *peregrinatio*), a holy war (*bellum sacrum* or *guerre sainte*), a passage or general passage (*passagium generale*), an expedition of the Cross (*expeditio crucis*) or the business of Jesus Christ (*negotium Jhesu Christi*): it is worth noticing how many of these terms were euphemisms. Only in the late twelfth century did the technical word *crucesignati*, signed with the Cross, come to be used of crusaders. At first they had simply been referred to as pilgrims and so they continued for centuries to be called, especially if they were campaigning to the East. But it is some comfort to recall that historians of feudalism have faced up to similar problems. They have not been deterred from making serious attempts to define a very important political, economic and social system which was subject to regional variations, lasted a long time and for which there was no concise contemporary term. Not surprisingly it is possible to describe feudalism in all sorts of different ways, but the important thing is that the attempts have been made and many of them have added greatly to our understanding of the Middle Ages.

Contemporaries, of course, knew perfectly well what a crusade was. How did they recognise one? In the writings of chroniclers, apologists and canon lawyers and in the wording of the phrases used by those who drew up papal encyclicals we can perceive the signs that informed the faithful that a crusade was being preached. First the participants, or some of them, were called upon to take the Cross, which is to say that they were to make a vow to join a military expedition with defined aims. The vow itself was of a special kind, and I shall have something to say about it later, but for the moment what is relevant is that at some kind of formal, public ceremony, which varied from place to place, men and women, rich and poor, priests and laymen, made a voluntary promise to take part in the campaign. We must, however, never think of a crusade as containing only crusaders, for their numbers, especially in some of the thirteenth-century expeditions, were often quite small: there were always many hangers-on and camp followers attached to an army while it became common for large numbers of professional soldiers to be employed and even for crusaders to travel East with sums of money with which to buy mercenaries. By the thirteenth century, moreover, many who took the Cross never actually departed on campaign. Practising what was known as substitution or redemption, which I will describe later, they sent another in their place or contributed sums of money instead of going, thus helping to finance an expedition. It is also important to note that not all crusades were the large, elaborately organised affairs which have rather inaccurately been given numbers by historians. They could be very small or made up of scattered bands of men departing at different times over several years: in certain periods, the 1170s or the later thirteenth century, much crusading took this form. The second sign that a crusade was being prepared was that those taking the Cross were answering a call that could only be made by the pope. Thirdly, in consequence of their vows and the performance of the actions promised the crusaders gained certain well-known privileges. These were subject to development and new rights were added to those originally granted, but we may say that all crusaders were assured that their families, interests and assets would be protected in their absence and that in the Indulgence they enjoyed a major spiritual privilege. The Indulgence could only be granted by the pope or his agents and it was references to it in papal encyclicals that really informed people that a crusade was being promoted.

A striking feature of the Indulgences granted to the participants in some of the military campaigns that took place in western Europe was that they were specifically associated with those given to crusaders going to recover Jerusalem or defend the Holy Land.

> We concede to all fighting firmly in this expedition the same remission of sins which we have given to the defenders of the Eastern Church. (Pope Calixtus II in 1123 concerning Spain)

To all those who do not receive the same Cross of Jerusalem and determine to go against the Slavs and remain in that expedition we concede... that remission of sins which our predecessor Pope Urban of happy memory instituted for those going to Jerusalem. (Pope Eugenius III in 1147 concerning Germany)

We wish that those men ... who take up arms to fight against the perfidious (the heretics) should enjoy that remission of sins which we have granted to those who labour in aid of the Holy Land. (Pope Innocent III in 1207, concerning the war against the Albigensians)

We grant the Indulgence ... to all those who undertake this labour personally or at their expense, and to those who do not personally participate but send suitable warriors at their own expense, according to their means and quality, and also to those who personally assume this burden at another's expense, and we wish them to enjoy that privilege and immunity which were conceded in the general council to those aiding the Holy Land.   (Pope Innocent IV in 1246, proclaiming war against the Emperor Frederick II)

We have thought it worthy to concede those Indulgences which in similar cases were accustomed to be given by the Holy See to those going to the aid of the Holy Land.   (Pope John XXII in 1326, concerning Spain)

Reading these and other grants of the Indulgence, it is clear that to the papal *Curia* many of the expeditions in Spain, along the shores of the Baltic, against heretics and schismatics and even against lay powers in Western Europe were to be regarded as belonging to the same species as crusades to the East. This is confirmed in the writings of the great canon lawyer Hostiensis (d.1271) and in the thirteenth-century practice of commutation, by which a man could change the terms of a vow made, say, to help the Holy Land into participation in a European campaign. It is quite impossible to agree with those historians who have accepted as crusades only the expeditions destined for Jerusalem or sent to the aid of Latin Palestine: we cannot ignore the fact that medieval men had a broader view of what they were than that. But we also have to take into account a number of campaigns authorised by the popes but waged by men who, although they had taken the Cross and were assured protection, enjoyed Indulgences not specifically equated with those given to the defenders of the East. Hostiensis seems to have considered that these were not true crusades and we can do little else but follow him, even though it should be stressed that the absence of a reference to the Holy Land in a papal encyclical is not certain evidence that no equation with the crusades to Palestine was intended – the Livonian Crusade of 1199 was certainly linked in the minds of contemporaries to those in the East, even though this was not made clear in the surviving authorisation of Pope Innocent III. And even in cases in which a distinction was the papal *Curia's* intention, it is hard to know how to categorise such expeditions, since the participants had taken the Cross and enjoyed protection.

To contemporaries a crusade was an expedition authorised by the pope, the leading participants in which took vows and consequently enjoyed the privileges of protection at home and the Indulgence, which, when the campaign was not destined for the East, was expressly equated with that granted to crusaders to the Holy Land. This enables us to identify what was regarded as a crusade, but it cannot take us much further. We can only find out what qualified an expedition for papal authorisation of this particular kind, allowing the crusaders taking part to make vows and enjoy the privileges, by examining the features common to those we have recognised as crusades. They were, of course, primarily wars, even though they might be said to have transcended war in that at times they were seen by their apologists as instruments of peace in the West, while the expeditions to the East, and many of those in the West as well, were viewed as pilgrimages. But all crusades were expected to conform to the principles underlying and to a certain extent limiting the bearing of arms by Christians and a useful approach, therefore, is to look at them against the background of Christian ideas on war.

If there are occasions on which war is justifiable, and since the early fifth century many have believed that there are such occasions, then we must admit that in certain circumstances the Fifth Commandment, enshrining a divine prohibition against homicide, can be set aside. But what are those circumstances? Traditionally, there have been two distinct answers to this question among those Christians who are not pacifists. The first, the most commonly held and, curiously, the only one really discussed by moral theologians today, is usually called the theory of the Just War. Its premise is that violence is always sinful, but

it recognises that, in intolerable conditions and provided that it is subject to stringent rules, war may be condoned by God. Early in the fifth
century St Augustine of Hippo, the first and still possibly the most
sophisticated Christian thinker on this matter, tried to define the
criteria to which war must accord before it could be considered to be
justifiable. These were later reduced, and greatly simplified, by
theologians and canon lawyers to three. First, the war must have a just
cause (*causa justa*) and normally such a cause could only be past or present aggression or injurious action by another. Secondly, it must rest on
what was known as the authority of the prince (*auctoritas principis*). In
other words it must be proclaimed by legitimate authority, usually, of
course, secular, although we will see that it was an ecclesiastic with
powers encompassing the authorisation of war who proclaimed a
crusade. Five centuries before the crusades these first two criteria had
been summed up by Isidore of Seville in a sentence which passed into
the collections of canon law: 'That war is lawful and just which is
waged upon command in order to recover property or to repel attack.'
The third criterion was known as right intention (*intentio recta*). Each of
the participants ought to have pure motives and war must be the only
apparently practicable means of achieving the justifiable purpose for
which it was to be fought.

The crusades, however, were expressions of another concept, that of
Holy War, in which force of arms is regarded as being not merely
justifiable and condoned by God, but positively sanctioned by him.
The subject has not had the attention from theologians and historians
that it deserves, but a starting point for discussion is that all Christian
writers who accept the notion of violence, whether justifiable or
sacred, recognise that it has not only a negative but also a positive side
to it. The waging of war is a political act, necessitated by events in this
world, and its positive aspect is therefore related to the needs of an im-
perfect natural order; it may, for instance, have the aim of restoring
that order or the *status quo*. Arguments for Just War go no further than
that. But the protagonists of Holy War, who invariably associate God
intimately with some political structure or course of political events in
this world, are led to believe that violence in support of that political
structure advances his intentions for mankind. War becomes more than
a necessary but unpleasant reaction to injustice or aggression; it is a
positive step in accordance with God's wishes, since it is fought on
behalf of a polity which itself is the product of his will. Holy Wars can
only be waged, as the great theologian Jacques Maritain recognised

forty years ago, when the temporal order and God's intentions become inextricably bound up with one another.

But a Holy War remains a Christian war and the conviction that it is holy does not exempt it from the limitations placed by traditional Christian thought on the use of violence. In particular, it must conform to the criteria of the just cause, the authority of the prince and right intention. Of course it would be absurd to suppose that all crusades had causes that reputable theologians would consider to be just or that all crusaders had pure motives, but aberrations do not invalidate what a crusade ought to have been, although studies of such matters certainly cast light on the practical application of the crusading ideal. Apologists were careful to write of the Indulgence being enjoyed only by those whose motives could not be impugned and went to great lengths to show how campaigns were justly caused, important above all because the crusaders were volunteers, not conscripts, and, like most men, would not generally participate in something obviously unjustifiable. This book is concerned with definition, not with judgements on the motives of individual crusaders or the worth of individual campaigns.

2 A Just Cause

A Just Cause for War

BY the middle of the thirteenth century Christian writers were generally in agreement that the just cause for a war must be defensive and their views prevail today. It is just to defend one's country, laws and traditional way of life, just to try to recover property unlawfully taken by another, perhaps even just to enforce by physical means a properly delivered judicial sentence. It is not just to wage a war of aggrandisement or of conversion. This principle, we shall see, applied to the crusade no less than to any war, but in the first century of the movement, when the just cause was still a subject of discussion, other justifications for crusading were being put forward. St Augustine's definition of a Just War, that it avenged injuries, presupposed a much less passive attitude on the part of the just than was later to be acceptable, especially in the notion of vengeance, which haunted canon lawyers until *c.* 1200, after which it seems gradually to have been dropped, and in a wide interpretation of the injuries to be avenged, which could include any violation of righteousness, God's laws or Christian doctrine. As late as the middle of the thirteenth century Hostiensis seems to have believed that Christendom had an intrinsic right to extend its sovereignty over all those who did not recognise the rule of the Roman Church or Roman Empire. Early on, moreover, there seems to have been some confusion as to whether or not the crusade could be waged as a war of conversion and at the time of the First Crusade some came perilously near to promoting it as such. One chronicler, Robert the Monk, made Pope Urban II at Clermont remind his audience of Charlemagne and Louis the Pious and other Frankish kings 'who destroyed the kingdoms of the pagans and incorporated them within the boundaries of Holy Church'. And, in a letter sent to the pope in 1098, after they had taken Antioch in Syria, the leaders of

the crusade wrote that they had fought against Turks and pagans but
not against heretics and begged Urban to come himself to eradicate all
heresies. The waging of a missionary war against the heathen, which
had long been an element in German thought, was a prominent theme
in 1147, during the preparations for a campaign against the pagans in
north-eastern Europe. The papal encyclical *Divina dispensatione,* which
authorised this German crusade, emphasised conversions, in this echoing St Bernard, responsible above all for the pope's support, who in his
letters utterly forbade any truce with the pagans 'until such time as,
with God's help, they shall be either converted or wiped out'. It should
be stressed that nowhere in *Divina dispensatione* did Pope Eugenius III
explicitly justify the crusade as a war of conversion and that St Bernard's approach was not as simple as the quotation given above would
suggest: to him the pagans directly threatened Christendom and it was
only because there was no alternative to the use of physical force that
they must be crushed if they would not be converted. But a close
association between missions and war was always a feature of the north
European crusades and it was in connection with one of them that a
pope made the most outspoken reference of all. In 1209 Innocent III encouraged the King of Denmark to take the Cross and share in the Indulgence granted to German crusaders 'to extirpate the error of
paganism and spread the frontiers of the Christian faith'. This was an
extraordinary statement, coming as it did from one of the greatest
canon lawyers and the leading apologist for the crusading movement
among the medieval popes, even though the letter did contain a
reference to the persecution of Christian preachers by the heathen and
one historian has considered that it was in accord with more conventional ideas. It may have been a momentary aberration on Innocent's
part or on that of some clerk in his *Curia,* but it is not the only curious
pronouncement that he made on the crusades. In 1201 he decreed that
such was the need of the Holy Land that a man could take the Cross
without his wife's assent. This ran counter to the traditional principles
of canon law on the binding and enduring consequences of the
marriage contract: that no one could unilaterally refuse his partner
marital rights without that partner's consent. It was an elementary mis-
take and later canon lawyers were careful to limit the exception to the
sole case of the interests of the Holy Land. Innocent's statements to the
King of Denmark and on a crusader's wife can perhaps only be understood in terms of his obsession with the crusading movement, an
obsession unequalled in any pope save Gregory X, which led him to

preach or authorise no fewer than six crusades. It is not surprising that
he overstepped the mark at times.

The opinions that vengeance for such injuries as the mere denial of
the Christian faith or the refusal to accept Christian government, and
the opportunity for conversion by force constituted just causes, were
those of minorities and were never held by most reputable Christian
thinkers, among whom it was generally agreed that non-Christians
could not be made to accept baptism nor could they be physically at-
tacked simply because they were of a different faith – although a distinction was drawn between Jews and Muslims, against the last of
whom force might be used only because they were already persecuting
Christians. The undercurrent of belief in the missionary crusade seems
to have weakened when the climate of opinion began to change
around 1200: the Church was now entering the Thomist age, with its
emphasis on the rights of the unconverted and on persuasion by means
of reason. In the middle of the thirteenth century Pope Innocent IV
authoritatively restated the conventional views. He asserted that infidels had rights in natural law and that a war of conversion was il-
legitimate; but he also argued that the Holy Land was rightfully Christian property, for it had been consecrated by the presence of Christ and
conquered by the Roman, later to be the Christian, Empire in a Just
War. As representative of Christ and heir of the emperors, the pope
could reassert Christian jurisdiction in Palestine and the crusades to the
East were merely recovering territory that rightfully belonged to
Christians. A Just War, moreover, could be launched to repel unjust
damage and as a punishment for sins; so the pope could proclaim a
crusade against a pagan ruler, not because he was pagan but because he
posed a threat to Christians or had sinned by, for instance, refusing to
allow Christian missionaries to operate in his territories. Innocent's influence can be seen working particularly clearly in the writings of
Hostiensis and in a treatise written by Humbert of Romans for Pope
Gregory X in the early 1270s. Humbert set out to answer those who
said that Christians should never take the initiative but were justified
only in defending themselves when the Muslims launched an attack
upon them. He replied that the Muslims were dangerous and sought
whenever they could to harm Christianity; they had seized lands once
in the possession of Christians and, moreover, they so openly consented
to iniquity that no Christian could ever be at peace with them without
incurring blame. The invasion of their lands was therefore justified and
he argued for attacks upon them to weaken their power, to reintroduce

the Christian faith in those lands from which it had been driven out and to express intolerance of sin. But he stressed that the crusade was not a war of aggression because its aim was the recovery of what had been Christian territory.

It has been suggested recently that it was only with Pope Innocent IV that the crusades, as Holy Wars, were truly made subject to the laws governing Just Wars. But in fact the traditional criteria for Just Wars, even if under discussion, had weighed heavily with apologists from the start. It is striking how consistently propaganda on behalf of the crusades – whether to the East or in Spain, along the shores of the Baltic, against heretics or Christian lay powers – justified them, and always had justified them, in terms of the recovery of property or of defence against aggression.

Crusades to the Near East

The just cause was in the mind of Pope Urban II when he preached the First Crusade. In the first week of March 1095 a council of bishops from France, Italy and Germany was in session at Piacenza. To it came an embassy from the Byzantine emperor Alexius I Comnenus appealing to the pope to encourage westerners to help defend the eastern Church against the Turks, who had swept through Asia Minor and had almost reached Constantinople. Urban replied with a sermon in which he urged men to help the emperor. His itinerary after Piacenza suggests that he was thinking of raising a small army to be sent to the East, perhaps under the captaincy of Count Raymond of Toulouse who had already been thought of by Pope Gregory VII for an expedition overseas, and certainly under the spiritual leadership of Adhémar of Monteil, Bishop of Le Puy, who may once have pilgrimaged to Jerusalem. After about a month at Piacenza Urban passed through northern Italy and on to France, whence he had come, accompanied by an impressive entourage which included four cardinals, two archbishops, several bishops and the great papal chancellor John of Gaeta, to favour the monastery of Cluny, where he had been prior, and to supervise the reform of the French Church. At Le Puy, the centre of Adhémar of Monteil's diocese, he issued a call to a council to be held at Clermont. By the end of August he was at S. Gilles, a favourite residence of Count Raymond of Toulouse, whom he may have met, for it seems that immediately after Urban had preached the crusade at

Clermont and far too soon for the news to have travelled south the count's envoys arrived to commit their master to the Cross. From S. Gilles the pope travelled slowly up the Rhône valley to Cluny, which he reached on about 18 October, staying at the monastery until the end of the month. On 14 November he was at Clermont and on the 18th the council opened. On the 27th, after the ecclesiastical business was finished, Urban preached the First Crusade to great crowds gathered outside the city in the open air and in a dramatic and obviously prearranged gesture Adhémar came forward first to take the Cross and to be appointed the pope's own representative in the army. Urban spent the eight months after Clermont preaching the Cross in western and southern France, but it soon became clear that the response to his call was very great, greater perhaps than he had anticipated. Late in December he wrote to Flanders, inviting its inhabitants to join. Early in February 1096 he commissioned two men to preach on his behalf in the Loire valley and in Normandy and England. From Pavia in September he wrote to those taking the Cross in Bologna and from Cremona in October he forbade the monks of Vallombrosa to participate.

It is hard now to fathom his mind. There survive reports of his sermon and his addresses to the clergy at Clermont written by four men who were probably present, but none was verbatim and all were written in the light of the success of the First Crusade. The surviving record of what the council of Clermont had to say on the crusade is based on notes taken by a bishop who was there. We have only three letters directly on the subject from Urban himself, the first written a month after the council. A slight inconsistency in these, a stress on the liberation of the eastern Churches and then a direct reference to the journey to Jerusalem, led to the suggestion, which has since become orthodox opinion, that, although the pope put forward Jerusalem as a goal to link the crusade with pilgrimages and to appeal to his listeners, his real purpose was the more limited one of fraternally answering the request of the Byzantine emperor for aid in the hope of bringing the Latin and Greek Churches closer to one another; it was his audience who took up the idea of the road to Jerusalem, originally a secondary, devotional aim, and fixed on it so that even before the crusade departed, the Holy City had become the primary objective. This interpretation has recently been challenged and it has been argued convincingly, on the evidence of chronicles and charters connected with the pope's preaching tour in France, that, although aid to the eastern

Christians and the union of the Churches were also aims, Jerusalem was uppermost in his mind from the start: the name of Jerusalem was far too potent to be used lightly, particularly by a reformer and ex-Cluniac like Urban. But whatever the uncertainty concerning the thoughts behind the preaching of the First Crusade there can be no doubts about its justification: there constantly recur in the sources the ideas of liberation (another word for recovery) and defence. The reports of Urban's sermons made him speak powerfully on the liberation of Jerusalem or the defence of the eastern Church; liberation is a theme of the canon of the council of Clermont on the crusade and of Urban's letters; and it is to be found in contemporary chronicles; an overwhelming weight of evidence suggests that the pope was proposing a war of reconquest, not of conquest.

With the taking of the Holy Land, of course, the justification for crusades to Palestine changed. The land consecrated by the presence of Christ was now in Christian hands and must be defended. Pope Eugenius III stressed this in 1145 and his words were echoed in later papal letters.

> By the grace of God and the zeal of your fathers, who strove to defend them over the years and to spread Christianity among the peoples in the area, these places have been held by Christians until now and other cities have courageously been taken from the infidel. . . .
>
> It will be seen as a great token of nobility and uprightness if those things which the efforts of your fathers acquired are vigorously defended by you, the sons. But if, God forbid, it comes to pass differently, then the bravery of the fathers will be shown to have diminished in the sons.

The city of Jerusalem was lost to Saladin in 1187 and was to be held by the Christians again only from 1229 to 1244. Of course its recapture came to be called for, although the burden of propaganda naturally rested on the need to defend what was left of the European settlement in the Holy Land. Even the invasion of Egypt, attempted in 1218 and 1249 and proposed at other times, was seen as contributing to the well-being of Latin Palestine. One chronicler made King John of Jerusalem in 1218 advise the invasion of Egypt to a council-of-war of the Fifth Crusade:

for if we could take one of these cities [of Alexandra and Damietta]
it is my opinion that by the use of it we could recover all of this
[Holy] land if we wanted to surrender it in exchange.

Since Egypt had been part of the Christian Roman Empire its conquest
could also be justified as the recovery of a once Christian land.

Crusades in Spain

For a long time there had been wars against the Moors in Spain when
Pope Urban II dissuaded Spaniards from joining the First Crusade and
gave them the right to an Indulgence, establishing an analogy between
the reconquests of the peninsula and Palestine. In 1100 and 1101 his
successor Paschal II also forbade Spaniards to go to the Holy Land and
granted an Indulgence to those who stayed behind to fight: he did not
want military success against the Moors jeopardised by the desertion of
warriors. From 1098 onwards the Indulgences given to Spaniards were
often equated with those granted to crusaders to Jerusalem and in 1123
the bishops at the First Lateran Council found it possible to refer to
those who took the Cross either for Jerusalem or for Spain, as though
both oaths were of the same sort. By the time of the Second Crusade a
contemporary could write of the Spanish army as being part of one
great host fighting on several fronts of Christendom.

Spain had once been Christian land, but great parts of it were subject
to infidels, who threatened the faithful in the North, and the Spanish
crusades, like those to the East, were consistently portrayed as being
defensive. In 1122 the foundation of the confraternity of Zaragoza was
made 'for the defence of Christians and the oppression of Muslims and
the liberty of Holy Church'.

Crusades in North-eastern Europe

In 1147, at the time when the Second Crusade was being prepared,
some German crusaders, mainly Saxons, wanted to campaign not in the
Orient but against the Slavs across the river Elbe. St Bernard, who was
in charge of the preaching of the Cross, agreed, perhaps because he saw
in Germany similarities to Spain. He seems to have acted on his own

initiative, only informing Pope Eugenius afterwards, but the pope concurred and a papal encyclical, *Divina dispensatione,* established the German crusade on the same lines as those in Spain and Palestine. North-eastern Europe had never been part of the Christian Empire and campaigning there could not be justified as the reconquest of Christian land. And it is difficult nowadays to envisage much of a threat being posed to Christendom by the backward Slav peoples: indeed at the time relations with them were getting better. But although there was, and always had been, an important missionary element in the German expeditions against their neighbours, care was also taken to justify them as defensive: *dilatio* and *defensio,* expansion and defence, went hand in hand. A good example of this can be found in a letter in which Pope Innocent III authorised the Livonian Crusade in 1199. To Innocent there had been persecution of Christian converts in Livonia by their pagan neighbours. An army must therefore be raised 'in defence of the Christians in those parts' and protection was promised to all who went 'to defend the Church of Livonia'.

Crusades against Schismatics and Heretics

Since very early times, the use of force against heretics had been considered justified. The canonist Gratian in *c.* 1140 had laid the foundations that were to enable the Church itself, rather than secular powers, to authorise such violence, but it was the Third Lateran Council in 1179 which first came near to proposing the launching of a crusade against heretics. The decrees of the council enjoined all the faithful for the remission of their sins to fight heresy and defend Christendom against it. It referred to such a war as a just labour, and stated that those taking part were to receive an Indulgence (although not automatically the plenary Indulgence) and were to be protected 'just like those who visit the Holy Sepulchre'. One result of the new decree was an extraordinary little expedition against the Albigensians under a papal legate early in the 1180s. But the crusade can be seen operating more certainly, with reference to schismatics, during the ill-fated Fourth Crusade which, originally aimed at either Palestine or Egypt, ended by taking the Christian city of Constantinople. Already in 1203, as the expedition veered inexorably off course, there was a section of the army which was arguing for an invasion of the Greek Empire 'because it is not subject to the Holy See and because the emperor of Constantinople usurped the imperial throne, having deposed and even blinded his brother'.

These justifications were again put forward in April 1204 when, after the emperors placed on the Byzantine throne by the western leaders had been murdered in a *coup d'état* inside Constantinople, the army was preparing for its final assault on the city. The Latin clergy preached sermons justifying the attack, and the burden of what they had to say was reported in almost identical passages by two of the eye-witnesses whose accounts have come down to us, Geoffrey of Villehardouin and Robert of Clari. The clergy

> showed to the barons and the pilgrims that he who was guilty of such a murder [of the emperors] had no right to hold land and all those who had consented were abettors of the murder; and beyond all this that they had withdrawn themselves from obedience to Rome. 'For which reasons we tell you,' said the clergy, 'that this war is lawful and just and that if you have a right intention to conquer this land and bring it into obedience to Rome all those who die after confession shall enjoy the Indulgence granted by the pope'.

It is interesting to find here an explicit reference to the crusade conforming to the criteria for a Just War. One of the arguments, it will be noted, was that political events in Constantinople constituted a sin, an offence which the crusade could punish – in 1203 Pope Innocent had commented that such things might be so but it was not for the crusaders to judge them nor had they assumed the Cross to vindicate this injury. The other argument was, as we should expect, that the Greeks were in schism, although the defensive nature of the operation was implicit rather than explicit. The same sort of reasoning can be perceived in Innocent's proclamation of the Albigensian Crusade. The date at which this crusade came into being is the subject of argument – perhaps it was as late as October 1208 – but already in 1204 the pope had written to the King of France encouraging him to take up arms in defence of the Church against the heretics and offering the same Indulgence as that granted to those who aided the Holy Land. In November 1207 he referred to the horrors of and threat from heresy which, he averred, must be dealt with as a doctor knifes a wound and, writing after the assassination of the papal legate, Peter of Castelnau, on 14 January 1208, he called on Philip of France to take up the shield of protection of the Church. In 1215 the Fourth Lateran Council repeated that the crusaders had the right to enjoy the same Indulgence as that given to defenders of the Holy Land. Similar justifications can be found on other occasions, for instance in the 1230s, when a crusade was launched in north Germany against the Stedinga peasants, who were regarded as heretics, and in the 1290s, when Pope Boniface VIII preached the Cross against the Colonnas, whom he portrayed as schismatics. However unattractive such reasoning may now appear to us, the crusades against heretics and schismatics were believed to be defensive. To Pope Innocent III in 1208 heretics were as bad as Muslims: they were a threat to Christendom, a threat, as Hostiensis put it, to catholic unity which was in fact more dangerous than that to the Holy Land.

Crusades against Lay Powers in the West

It has often been argued, and indeed was said by some in the thirteenth century, that the least justifiable crusades were those launched against secular opponents of the papacy in western Europe. But, again, they were justified in the traditional way; Hostiensis, indeed, was to suggest that there were no differences between the 'disobedient' and schismatics and heretics. To some historians the original 'political crusade' was that led in 1106 by Bohemond of Antioch against the Greeks, but as far as we can tell it was preached in terms of an expedition to Jerusalem, and it is more likely that the first true crusade against a Christian layman was that proclaimed by Innocent III against Markward of Anweiler. Markward was one of the lieutenants of the Emperor Henry VI, who, after the emperor's death, tried to keep control of the March of Ancona and later to seize the regency of the Kingdom of Sicily, harassing that set up by the pope for Henry's young son Frederick II. Innocent, who was preparing the Fourth Crusade, responded by preaching the Cross against Markward whom he claimed was in practice allied to the Muslims.

> We concede to all who fight the violence of Markward and his men the same remission of sins that we concede to all who go against the perfidy of the Muslims in defence of the eastern provinces, because through him aid to the Holy Land is impeded.

The pope was, in fact, proclaiming one crusade in support of another that was being prepared: Markward's actions were menacing the help

that was to be sent to the Holy Land and in this way he posed the same
threat as did the Muslims. The organisation of the campaign was very
indecisive – it has recently been shown that it was a measure of
desperation when all else had failed – and in 1203 Markward deprived
it of reason by dying, but the same train of thought can be seen in the
Ad Liberandum constitution of the Fourth Lateran Council in 1215, according to which those who broke the peace in Europe during the
crusade, holding

> ecclesiastical censure in little esteem, can fear, not without reason,
> lest by the authority of the Church secular power be brought in
> against them, as those disturbing the business of the Crucified
> One, . . .

and probably in Clement IV's authorisation of a crusade in 1265 against
the rebellious English nobles.

The next move was made by Pope Gregory IX, not in 1228–30
when his campaign against the Emperor Frederick II was certainly not
a crusade and should be compared more with the steps taken to defend
the papacy in the eleventh century, but in 1240. War had broken out
again and Frederick was now threatening the city of Rome itself. In
Rome Gregory publicly exhibited the holiest relics, the heads of SS
Peter and Paul, distributed crosses and called on the populace to defend
the liberty of the Church. The papal legate in Milan was permitted to
preach the Cross in order to raise an army in Lombardy and crusade
preaching was also authorised in Germany. A letter sent to Hungary in
February 1241 listed the benefits to be granted to those taking the
Cross: they were to enjoy the same Indulgence as that given to
crusaders to the Holy Land; redemptions of vows were allowed and so
were commutations to the campaign against Frederick of vows
originally made for defence of Palestine. The defensive nature of the
war was emphasised: Gregory pointed out that Christianity was 'in
such peril' that military action had become necessary and he referred to
the 'vows of the crusaders in defence of the Church against Frederick'.
Justification in terms of defence, indeed, characterised all the appeals
for the crusades against lay powers in the West: for instance in 1246 a
new crusade against Frederick II was proclaimed for the defence of the
catholic faith and the liberty of the Church and the crusade against
King Peter of Aragon in 1284 was preached 'in defence of the catholic
faith and also the Holy Land'.

A Cause for a Crusade

A crusade, whenever and against whomsoever it was aimed, was regarded as being essentially defensive and thus conformed to the basic principle of the just cause. Of course it has never been beyond the wit of man plausibly to excuse his actions, presenting them in the best possible light by calling attention to a threat that does not really exist, but it is undeniable that the just cause had important effects on the movement. A pope might proclaim a crusade, but success depended, as many popes found to their cost, not only on the papal call but also on the answer of the faithful to it. Men took the Cross for all kinds of motive, bad as well as good, but the doubts of ordinary people worried apologists and theoreticians like Hostiensis and in an idealistic age there could be no lasting appeal that did not have some clear justification. A just cause, therefore, was needed and it was bound to be a limiting factor, for a crusade had to be presented as a reaction to what others had done. The initiative had to lie with the enemy and a crusade was often merely a ponderously slow response to what he did.

As far as the cause for them was concerned the crusades did more than conform to the traditional criterion for a Just War; as Holy Wars they also had special features. The recovery of property or defence was related not to a particular country or empire but to Christendom at large, to the Church or to Christ himself. It was not the property of the Byzantine Empire or of the Kingdom of Jerusalem that was liberated or defended by the crusades to the East, but territory belonging by right to Christendom or to Christ. It was not Spaniards or Germans, but Christians, who were imperilled by the Moors and Slavs. The Albigensians menaced not so much France, nor Frederick II the papal patrimony, as they threatened the Church.

To understand this attitude we must take into account the political philosophy which dominated western European thought at the time. Christendom had many meanings, but in political terms it was seen not merely as a society of Christians but as a universal state, the Christian Republic, transcendental in that it existed at the same time in heaven and on earth. Providing the political context in which man could fully develop his potential for loving God and his neighbour, it was the only true sovereign state. Earthly kingdoms had no real political validity, being at best temporal conveniences which could be treated as its provinces. It had its possessions and its citizens. Any asset — such as territory once governed by Christians but now in the hands of outsiders – could be restored to its rule; any threat to its subjects, whether from without or within, must be resisted. A crusade was its army, fighting in its defence or for the recovery of property lost by it. The leaders of the First Crusade could write of the spreading of 'the kingdom of Christ and the Church'; and St Bernard could argue that the cause of King Louis VII of France, setting out for the East, was of importance not only to him 'but to the whole Church of God, because now your cause is one with that of all the world'. A century later Odo of Châteauroux made the same point in one of his sermons.

> But someone says, 'The Muslims have not hurt me at all. Why should I take the Cross against them?' But if he thought well about it he would understand that the Muslims do great injury to every Christian.

And in the late 1140s, when crusades were being fought at the same time on several fronts, they were seen as regiments in one Christian army.

> To the initiators of the expedition [wrote a German chronicler] it seemed that one part of the army should be sent to the eastern regions, another into Spain and a third against the Slavs who live next to us.

The universal Christian state was a monarchy, founded and ruled over by Christ, for whom in this world popes, bishops and kings acted as agents. Enemies of the commonwealth were the enemies of its king. Writers at the time of the First Crusade referred to the Muslims in the East as the 'enemies of God' and in one report of his sermon Urban II was made to say: 'It is not I who encourages you, it is the Lord. . . . To those present I say, to those absent I command, but Christ rules.' He hailed the crusaders as 'soldiers of Christ', while they wrote of themselves as 'the army of the Lord'. To Innocent III the crusade was an enterprise which was particularly Christ's own and those who aided the Muslims were acting against the 'interests of Christ himself and the Christian people'.

It was because of the special nature of its cause and its association with a political order established for the good of mankind by Christ that the crusade was not merely justifiable but was holy. Participation in it was especially meritorious. Of course it is the case that participation in a Just War can be in a way an act of merit, in the performance, for instance, of a patriotic service. But it can never be anything but inherently sinful, whereas the taking of the Cross was demanded as a religious duty, and one for which the layman was particularly qualified. The great preacher James of Vitry spoke of the crusade as being incumbent on the Christian as military service was upon a vassal.

> When a lord is afflicted by the loss of his patrimony he wishes to prove his friends and find out if his vassals are faithful. Whoever holds a fief of a liege lord is worthily deprived of it if he deserts him when he is engaged in battle and loses his inheritance. You hold your body and soul and whatever you have from the Supreme Emperor and today he has had you called upon to help him in battle; and though you are not bound by feudal law, he offers you so many and such good things, the remission of all sins, whatever the penalty or guilt, and above all eternal life, that you ought at once to hurry to him.

From the ninth century a new path to martyrdom, dying in the war against the infidel, had been officially spoken of and in the eleventh century there had come the concept of the remission of the sins of warriors in a good cause and the idea of the soldier of Christ at the special disposal of the papacy. With Pope Urban II the crusade was proposed as a positive act of virtue, a means of Grace, an expression of love both of God, for whom one fought, and of one's neighbours in the eastern Churches, whom one was striving to liberate. And, because he saw it as linked to the Truces of God by which the Church was trying to impose some sort of peace in France, Urban stressed – references appear in all the reports of his sermons – the difference between the old unregenerate knight, who quarrelled with his neighbours, and the new knight, who fought for such a worthy cause.

> Now become soldiers of Christ [he was reported as saying] you who a little while ago were robbers. Now legally fight against barbarians, you who once fought against brothers and blood-relatives. . . . Those who were the enemies of the Lord, now these will be his friends.

The idea expressed here was not new, but its impact on audiences is borne out by the way it was reiterated by preachers for a century. St

Bernard, in particular, concentrated on it. To him the old knight committed homicide, whether he lived or died, prevailed or was conquered; the new knight killed not man, but evil.

> For how long will your men continue to shed Christian blood; for how long will they continue to fight amongst themselves? You attack one another, you slay one another and by one another you are slain. What is this savage craving of yours? Put a stop to it now, for it is not fighting but foolery. So to risk both soul and body is not brave but shocking, is not strength but folly. But now O mighty soldiers, O men of war, you have a cause for which you can fight without danger to your souls; a cause in which to conquer is glorious and for which to die is gain.

The knights of Christ fought in expiation of their sins and as a means to their salvation. They were, in the Old Testament imagery constantly used of them, the elect, the Israelites crossing the Red Sea. They were expected to conform to such standards of behaviour and dress as were suitable for members of the Lord's host. From 1145 onwards papal and lay decrees for crusaders contained what are known as sumptuary clauses demanding simplicity of dress and temperance in daily life.

> And if at any time the crusaders should lapse into sin, may they soon rise again through true penitence, having humility in heart and body, following moderation both in clothing and in food, shunning altogether quarrels and envy, banishing inward rancour and anger, so that, fortified with spiritual and material weapons, they may do battle with the enemy, more secure in faith, not presuming on their own power but trusting in Divine strength.

And death, they were told over and over again in sermons, tracts and chronicles, was martyrdom. The prospect of immediate entry into paradise was constantly held before them by propagandists like St Bernard.

> Go forward then in security, knights, and drive off without fear the enemies of the Cross of Christ, certain that neither death nor life can separate you from the love of God which is in Jesus Christ. . . . How glorious are those who return victorious from the battle! How happy are those who die as martyrs in the battle! Rejoice, courageous

athlete, if you survive and are victor in the Lord; but rejoice and glory the more if you die and are joined to the Lord. For your life is fruitful and your victory glorious. But death. . . is more fruitful and more glorious. For if those who die in the Lord are blessed, how much more so are those who die for the Lord!

The crusade, therefore, conformed to the principle of the Just War in that it was concerned above all with the recovery of lost lands and with defence. But as a Holy War its cause related to the Church, to Christendom, seen as a political entity, and to Christ, the monarch of the universal Christian state. It is not surprising that it was regarded as a means of salvation for those taking part, who were doing their duty by Christ as they might by their temporal lord or king.

3 Legitimate Authority

Papal Authorisation

CHRISTIANS are faced with the problem of reconciling the demands on the individual of love with the apparent need in a sinful world to use force. St Augustine's answer has proved itself to be generally acceptable. In a private capacity no man ought ever to kill, even in his own defence; but he may be justified in doing so as a public duty. Public warfare, as opposed to personal acts of violence, must be legitimised by public authority. It follows that a Just or Holy War must be authorised by a ruler whose powers are normally considered to include the right to proclaim it. A difference between crusades and other Holy Wars was that the ruler who legitimised them was not an emperor or king, but the pope; and resulting from the papal initiative were the characteristic privileges enjoyed by crusaders, particularly the Indulgence, which could be granted only by him.

The way in which popes came to proclaim crusades was established by two of them: Urban II, who set the precedent when he preached the First Crusade in 1095; and Eugenius III, who issued for the Second Crusade *Quantum predecessores,* the first true crusade encyclical. Whatever the contribution of Pope Gregory VII to crusading ideas – and I shall touch on that question later – the initiative following the appeal of the Byzantine embassy to the Council of Piacenza was Urban's own. Many of the elements to be found in the writings connected with his visit to France – the criteria for war, and especially Holy War, the pilgrimage and the pilgrim's vow, the Truce of God, the concept of the Christian Republic – were old, but it was he who synthesised them into what was recognisably a crusade, giving the expedition a theoretical basis which was to prove itself to be extraordinarily long-lasting. He was, as one of the chroniclers put it, the 'chief author of the expedition' and he regarded it as his own. 'We have constituted our most beloved son Adhémar, Bishop of Le Puy, leader in our place of this pilgrimage and labour.' The acceptance of papal headship was expressed especially clearly in a letter written to Urban by the captains of the crusade in September 1098. They informed him of the death of Adhémar, 'whom you gave us as your vicar,' and they went on:

> Now we ask you, our spiritual father, who started this journey and caused us all by your sermons to leave our lands . . . to come to us and summon whomsoever you can to come with you. . .

What could be better than that

> you who are the father and head of the Christian religion should come to the chief and capital city of the name of Christ and yourself finish off the war *which is your own* . . . . If indeed you come to us and with us complete the journey begun through you all the world will be obedient to you.

The half century that divided the First and Second Crusades was a period in which histories and chronicles told the story of the success of Urban's enterprise; men pilgrimaged, or at least looked with pride and devotion, towards Jerusalem now that it was in Latin hands; Urban's successors tried to help the new Latin colony in the Holy Land; and St Bernard began to develop in his preaching and writing the theory of crusading. But on Christmas Eve 1144 the Muslims broke into the city of Edessa in northern Mesopotamia, the capital of the first Latin Christian county to be established in the wake of the First Crusade. The news of the disaster, the first real setback for the Latins in the East, caused a great stir in the West, but what then happened is still rather mysterious. On 1 December 1145 Pope Eugenius III issued the encyclical *Quantum predecessores,* but although this was addressed to King Louis VII and the nobility of France there is no evidence that it was published there. Meanwhile Louis was already planning to lead a French expedition to the Holy Land: it may be that the pope issued *Quantum predecessores* because he had heard of this, for Louis does not seem to have envisaged seeking papal authorisation when he announced his idea to the Christmas court held at Bourges. His proposal met with little response and his chief adviser Suger of S. Denis was against it. Louis postponed a final decision until the following Easter and called for an opinion from St Bernard, who declared that he would not consider anything without consulting the pope. The result was that on 1 March 1146 *Quantum predecessores* was reissued, with a very slight change in the text which does not concern us here.

The story of the publication of *Quantum predecessores* demonstrates two things. The first is that initiative did not always lie with the papacy. Louis VII was one of several leaders of major and minor expeditions (perhaps the most famous being his great-grandson Louis IX) who themselves took the Cross without prompting from Rome. The second is that, whoever was responsible for the first move, papal authorisation was considered to be essential at some stage: not only great passages but also the tiny enterprises that were, increasingly after 1250, to depart backed by papal appeals and fortified by papal privileges were authorised by papal letters. At first sight an exception might be found in some canonists' treatment of crusades against heretics. They argued that a general authority to princes had already been given by the Fourth Lateran Council and that therefore no special papal edict was required before the waging of war against them. But this, one must stress, was only because it was considered that papal authorisation had already been granted. *Quantum predecessores* itself recounted how Urban,

> sounding forth as a heavenly trumpet, summoned sons of the Holy Roman Church from several parts of the world to free the eastern Church.

It went on:

> And so in the Lord we impress upon, ask and order all of you, and we enjoin it for the remission of sins, that those who are on God's side, and especially the more powerful and the nobles, vigorously equip themselves to go against the multitude of the infidels.

The encyclical also established the form in which crusades would thenceforward be proclaimed. The way the papal letters were written developed over the years, their style became more flowery and more dense and they are a good guide to the progress of crusading ideas, but they kept to the pattern laid down by *Quantum predecessores,* consisting of sections in which the circumstances that made a new crusade necessary were described, the appeal for crusaders was made and the privileges to be granted to participants and supporters were listed. The greatest of them were the bulls of Innocent III's pontificate, *Post miserabile* (1198), *Ne nos ejus* (1208) and *Quia major* (1213), which together with the great constitution *Ad Liberandum* of the Fourth Lateran Council (1215) contain the most marvellous language and imagery. And in practically every word papal authority is made clear.

> But to those declining to take part, if indeed there be by chance such men ungrateful to the Lord our God, we firmly state on behalf of the Apostle that they should know that they will have to reply to us on this matter in the presence of the Dreadful Judge on the Last Day of Severe Judgement.

We will see how unreal these pretensions were when it actually came to directing the course of a crusade.

A feature of Christianity is that, although it teaches that all man's actions are answerable to God and subject to the objective scale of values embodied in his laws, it divides governmental functions in this world into two distinct fields, the spiritual and the temporal. This separation of functions is to be found very early, even though there have been periods in which the boundary between them was indistinct or in which some institution – Late Roman emperorship, the thirteenth-century papacy, Anglican kingship – has been thought to transcend that boundary. In spite of, and paradoxically also because of, papal claims, at no period was the distinction between temporal and spiritual spheres of activity stressed more than during the central Middle Ages.

If ever there was a secular activity it is war and it is natural that in Christian history its prosecution or the physical repression of heresy should have been regarded as the duties of temporal rulers, emperors and kings. How then could a churchman like the pope authorise so secular an enterprise? We shall never understand the papal role in the crusading movement without first grasping the paradox that the popes were at the same time maintaining that the Church must run her own affairs freed from the control of lay rulers and that they, as the most responsible ministers of Christ in the earthly part of the Christian Republic, had some measure of authority on his behalf in temporal matters.

These contradictory claims had been made with great force during the Investiture Contest, which had begun as a dispute over church order and reform but had rapidly escalated so that in 1076 and 1080

Pope Gregory VII had provisionally and then definitively deposed King Henry IV of Germany. In trying to remove a man from an indisputably secular office the pope had stepped across the frontier that divided spiritual from temporal jurisdiction. In the past, it is true, popes had claimed superiority to emperors, but the origin of the imperial office in the West lay in a coronation performed by a pope on Christmas Day 800 and the emperors had duties which could be interpreted as making them merely agents of the Church. It was another matter with western kingship, which had grown up out of the fragmentation of the Roman Empire, owing little to the papacy, and had always been seen as a separate ministry for God. There were, moreover, no real precedents for papal intervention in the exercise of royal government other than the doubtful authorisation by Pope Zacharias of the removal from office of King Childeric of the Franks in the middle of the eighth century. Gregory VII's deposition of Henry IV was an extreme act which might be said to have been in advance of the development of papal theory – too advanced to be properly understood or appreciated by contemporaries – and at the time it was a failure in that Gregory was driven from Rome by Henry's forces and in 1085 died in exile. He was succeeded by Victor III and then in 1088 by Urban II, himself a strong Gregorian.

The great quarrel with the King of Germany went on and when Urban began his pontificate few German bishops recognised him and much of Germany and north and central Italy, including Rome, were controlled by Henry's anti-pope, Clement III. Urban set out to build up support for himself in the West and from Byzantium. By 1094 Rome was in his hands and the German king was losing ground in Italy; and in 1095, as the pope journeyed to France after the Council of Piacenza, Henry's son Conrad, who had rebelled against his father, became his vassal at Cremona. Against this background his preaching of the First Crusade had a political significance. It was an important move in the Investiture Contest, for when he called on the army of Christ to recover Christian land Urban was in fact assuming for himself the imperial function of directing the defence of the Christian Republic at a time when he did not recognise Henry as emperor. Gregory VII had deposed a king; Urban II took over the prime duty of a temporal ruler. With these actions the popes began to take a special place for themselves at the summit of both jurisdictions.

Although it took some time for political thinkers and canon lawyers to catch up with the ideas expressed in the deposition of Henry IV and the preaching of the First Crusade these foreshadowed what is known as the Papal Monarchy. By the early thirteenth century the pope was claimed to be Christ's Vicar, a special representative unlike any other earthly ruler, the Ordinary Judge of all things with a plenitude of power, standing in an intermediate position between God and the two hierarchies of ecclesiastical and temporal ministers. But even with the full development of the theory the popes' powers were less than absolute. In the first place the co-operative nature of the relationship between papal and temporal authority was still recognised: kings had their own share of government, holding a ministry for God in the exercise of which the pope would not normally interfere, for his court remained that of final appeal with an authority that could be invoked only in the last resort. Secondly, secular rulers could always act in ways in which popes would, perhaps could, not. The processes of papal jurisdiction, which were of course ecclesiastical, were not suited – and it was never pretended that they were – to the settlement of cases in temporal law. Thirdly, the popes really had no means of enforcing secular judgements even had they wanted to, for they had no effective means of imposing secular sentences. This can be seen clearly if one compares the reality of their government of the Church with the shadow of their government of the world. If there is one outstanding feature of the papacy in the central Middle Ages it is the way it gained direct control of and elaborated the administrative apparatus of the Church. The period saw great development of the whole machinery of government: of officials, courts and canon law, and the subordination of all, though never in practice quite as completely as a glance at structure would suggest, to Rome's will. But turning to the popes' relationship with the world, we find no such machinery. A pope like Innocent IV could solemnly depose a recalcitrant ruler like Frederick II, but he could only enforce his decision by resorting to the ecclesiastical apparatus, perhaps by threatening all Frederick's supporters with an ecclesiastical sanction like excommunication. Or he could launch a crusade.

It is not surprising that the papacy should look for means by which the temporal world, so alien to itself, could be adapted to its own processes of government. An example of this can be seen in Innocent III's decretal *Novit,* which justified papal interference in temporal matters *ratione peccati,* by reason of the sin involved in them. It has often been pointed out that since sin is potentially present in almost every human act this more or less gave the pope a blank cheque to intervene whenever and in whatever case he liked. But far more important than that – indeed it was to lead to problems of interpretation later – were the legal consequences of the transfer of a case *ratione peccati* to papal jurisdiction. Now a moral question, it became subject to the ordinary processes of ecclesiastical law and jurisdiction: in other words a temporal matter had become legally spiritual and had passed into a field in which the pope could properly operate. The crusade was another example of the same approach. A crusader was a soldier, but of a special kind, for he had taken a vow, *ipso facto* a spiritual matter, which resulted in his having the status of a pilgrim and consequently becoming, like a pilgrim, a temporary ecclesiastic, subject to church courts. The crusade vow, therefore, had a significance which was certainly clear by the middle of the twelfth century when the right of crusaders to answer cases in ecclesiastical courts was referred to. Of course secular courts were reluctant to agree to a reduction in their rights of jurisdiction and it came to be accepted that crusaders should answer to them on feudal tenures, inheritance and major crimes; but the principle was accepted and the crusader, although engaged in a secular activity, was incorporated into the system in which papal power freely worked. By the introduction of the vow and the granting of pilgrim status Urban II had created the conditions in which the pope could have authority over a crusade and use with regard to it the existing machinery of church government.

There was another side to this, for everything, including subjection in this matter to the control of the ecclesiastical apparatus, depended on vows being taken. When a pope proclaimed a crusade, this was no more than an appeal to the faithful to take the vow, which was essentially voluntary. He might threaten them with hell-fire but he could not make them take it or punish them if they did not. Without their fervour he could do nothing. It took, therefore, more than a pope to make a crusade. In the absence of a lay ruler's initiative, there had to be an adequate response to a papal appeal, and there were periods, particularly from 1150 to 1187, before the annihilation of the Christian army at the Battle of Hattin and the loss of the city of Jerusalem at last awoke the West, during which the papacy and Christian leaders in the East tried again and again with very little success to raise help for Palestine. In fact the difficulties encountered by popes in getting crusades off the ground were daunting. In order to maximise the benefits of whatever response there might be, peace had to be made to prevail in Europe; agents had to be appointed to publicise the appeal

and organise recruitment; and finance, increasingly important as time
went on, had to be raised.

Peace in Christendom

Long tradition associated the Christian Republic with peace. To St
Augustine, on whose writings the idea of the universal Christian state
was rather inaccurately based, peace was a distinguishing feature of the
true state, the City of God. The crusade itself was from the first seen as
an instrument of peace, closely associated with the movement for
Truces of God: it is clear that Urban II hoped to direct the bellicosity
of French knights overseas, bringing a measure of calm to the coun-
tryside. In the twelfth and thirteenth centuries it was believed that
peace in Europe and the unity of Christendom were essential precon-
ditions for the success of a crusade; and calls, often with reason, for
truces and unity are to be found again and again in papal letters: persis-
tent rivalry between the kings of France and England certainly
hindered the raising of a crusade in the 1170s and 1180s. The appeals
reached a climax with Pope Innocent III. To him the disunity of
Christendom was a shameful scandal and after 1204 he believed that on
the reform of a Church now united by the capture of Constantinople
depended the reconquest of Jerusalem. He felt as deeply about political
disputes in western Europe, even, as we have seen, preaching the Cross
against Markward of Anweiler for impeding a crusade and threatening
others with the same fate. In the preamble to the encyclical of 1198
which proclaimed the Fourth Crusade he seethed with powerful in-
dignation, in a voice not heard since that of St Bernard.

> Now indeed . . .while our princes pursue one another with inex-
> orable hatred, while each strives to vindicate his injuries, suffered at
> the hands of another, there is no one who is moved at the injury suf-
> fered by the Crucified One . . . ..Already our enemies insult us, say-
> ing, 'Where is your God, who cannot free himself or you from our
> hands?'

The calls of the popes for peace and unity were never very successful
and indeed the eventual failure of the crusades to hold the Holy Land
has been attributed partly to the growing disinclination in the later
thirteenth century of western powers, deeply involved in their own

rivalries, to participate. This is an exaggeration of the true situation, but it is clear that by the 1270s the papacy was beginning to realise the futility of trying to organise a great expedition at a time when kings had their minds on other matters.

Preaching

No papal proclamation after the first was itself enough to move Europe. Encyclicals had to be followed up by personal visits and constant publicity, a process known as the preaching of the Cross. It was obviously important that the popes should have control over this and therefore over recruitment. It might be supposed that they would have been only too happy with an enthusiastic response – or sometimes indeed with any reaction at all – and it is true that Innocent III and his successors tried to make their preachers' tasks easier by granting Indulgences even to those who merely listened to their sermons; it is a measure of the difficulties faced by the propagandists that the amount of Indulgence given to the audiences at crusade sermons was steadily increased as the thirteenth century wore on. But in fact there were occasions on which almost as bad for Rome as indifference in the West was the overenthusiasm of men whom the popes wanted to remain at home. Urban II may not have envisaged the uncontrollably large numbers who responded to his sermon at Clermont and he and his successors tried, sometimes unsuccessfully, to dissuade Spaniards from leaving the struggle in Spain and going East. Eugenius III did not want Conrad of Germany to take part in the Second Crusade but could do little to prevent him. In 1198 Innocent III seems to have had no desire for the participation in the Fourth Crusade of European monarchs, after the quarrelling and rivalries displayed on the Third and what may have been an effort by the Staufen emperors to seize control of the movement; he was lucky in that no king felt constrained to join. The matter was delicate in that it can be shown that often the response of ordinary knights to the preaching depended on the enthusiasm or indifference of the king or great magnates in a particular area.

In fact preaching was never completely controlled by the papacy. The central Middle Ages had many popular evangelisers and these have an important place in the history of the crusades. The most famous of them, Peter the Hermit, was active in central France and the Rhineland in 1095–6 and was followed East by an army of the poor, travelling independently of the other bands of crusaders, which was decimated by the Turks in western Asia Minor although Peter himself and the remnants of his followers were still to play a significant part at Antioch in northern Syria in 1098. Among his successors were Rudolph, a Cistercian monk whose influence in the Rhineland worried St Bernard at the time of the Second Crusade; Nicholas, the boy who launched the pathetic and misnamed Children's Crusade in 1212; and the Master of Hungary, the preacher of the Crusade of the Shepherds in 1251. The sermons of these men dwelt on those messianic, visionary themes with the emphasis on the rewards of the poor that characterised the populist movement which underlay the crusades and occasionally erupted in migrations towards the Promised Land, which was believed to be a paradise only the underprivileged could acquire.

A far greater part, however, was played by the official propagandists among whom were, of course, the popes themselves. We have already seen Urban II following up his call at Clermont by touring western and southern France. In 1215 Innocent III opened the Fourth Lateran Council with a sermon which partly concerned the crusade and in 1216 he preached the Cross in central Italy; at Orvieto, as at Clermont 120 years before, the crowds were so great that he addressed them in the open air, in spite of the heavy rain. In 1274 Gregory X referred to the crusade in at least three sermons at the Second Council of Lyons. But the popes could not, with their responsibilities and commitments, engage in many personal appearances and they had to rely on agents, most commonly, of course, local bishops. At Clermont Urban II urged the bishops to preach the Cross and in December 1099 Paschal II asked the French bishops to encourage knights to go to the Holy Land and especially to compel those who had already taken the Cross: there survives a letter, written by the Archbishop of Rheims to a suffragan, announcing the fall of Jerusalem to the crusaders and ordering that in all parishes there should be prayers for victory, fasting and the collection of alms. Throughout the period of the crusades a stream of letters flowed from the papal *Curia*, ordering bishops to preach the Cross themselves or help those sent by the popes to do so; and it seems that by the 1180s, at least in Britain, the prelates had with the assistance of the lesser clergy developed a fairly systematic procedure for crusade preaching.

The papacy also employed special agents. In February 1096 Urban II gave Robert of Arbrissel, who was later to found Fontevrault, commission to preach the Cross in the Loire valley and he ordered Gerento,

Abbot of S. Bénigne of Dijon, to publicise the crusade in Normandy and England. In 1100 Paschal II sent to France two cardinals who held a council at Poitiers and encouraged the faithful to join a crusade to the East. The best known of the early agents was St Bernard, who was employed by Pope Eugenius III to preach the Second Crusade in France and was forced, because of Rudolph's success, to extend his activities to Germany. The terms of Bernard's commission are not clear: he was certainly not a papal legate, and so could not have been given powers to act in this matter as if he were the pope himself, although the success of his preaching, the force of his personality and influence he had with Eugenius clearly gave him a very great authority. The first use of legates in the preaching of the Cross appears to have been in 1173–4 and from then on they were often employed.

A new development came with Innocent III's pontificate. He combined the use of special agents and provincial clergy by appointing local churchmen as his representatives. In 1198, when he proclaimed the Fourth Crusade, a legate was sent to France and free-lancers like the famous preacher Fulk of Neuilly were allowed to operate, but also two men in each province were chosen from among the higher clergy to preach the Cross together with a Templar and a Hospitaller. In 1208, when he tried, at least in France and Lombardy, unsuccessfully to promote a new crusade, he proposed to use much the same system, but in 1213 he introduced a more elaborate one. He himself kept an eye on the preaching in Italy, but for nearly every province in Christendom he also appointed small groups of men – the numbers varied slightly – many of whom were bishops. Innocent referred to them as executors, with the powers of legates in this matter, and he laid down that they should live modestly, being accompanied by only a few servants; they should preach, receive vows and, if given any donation for the Holy Land, store it in a religious house; they could appoint deputies in each diocese: in Liège and Cologne four of these were chosen – and the pope advised the Bishop of Ratisbon to appoint deputies who could assemble the populace of two or three parishes to address them where they could not deal with them individually. Perhaps the most successful of the executors was Oliver, the *scholasticus* of Cologne, whose preaching in that province, sometimes accompanied, it was said, by miracles, aroused great enthusiasm. Outside the scheme lay Hungary, where every bishop was to preach the Cross; Latin Syria and Palestine, where James of Vitry, the new Bishop of Acre and the greatest preacher of the day, was to raise crusaders; Denmark and Sweden, where the legate, the Archbishop of Lund, was to be assisted by the Archbishop of Uppsala; and France, to which papal legates, first Robert of Courçon and later Archbishop Simon of Tyre, were sent. This elaborate, perhaps overelaborate, structure does not seem to have been used again with regard to all Christendom, although, as in 1234, its details might be repeated in individual provinces. On other occasions prelates might be asked to preach themselves or to choose men to do so, or groups of clergy, like the Franciscans and Dominicans in the 1230s, might be directly appointed to publicise the crusades. There was, however, a tendency to give individual preachers the legation and wide powers. Examples are Conrad of Porto in Germany and Italy in the 1220s, Odo of Châteauroux in France and Germany in the 1240s and Ottobuono Fieschi over Norway, Flanders, Gascony, Britain and Ireland in 1265. Ottobuono had authority to appoint subordinate preachers, notaries and collectors; he preached some sermons himself, but generally delegated powers to whomsoever he thought fit, especially local friars.

Finance

Crusades were expensive and tended to become more so as the mercenary element in them increased. The costs of equipment, supplies and above all transport – most went by sea – were often too heavy for the participants; in 1202 the crusaders in Venice found themselves quite unable to pay for shipping that had been arranged for many more men than had actually arrived at the port of embarkation. It was quite usual for kings or the greater lords to pay inducements to or a part of the expenses of those of their followers who took the Cross. The total cost of the crusade of 1248–54 to King Louis IX of France was estimated at 1,537,570 *livres* or more than six times his annual income; and this was certainly an underestimate as it can been shown that he spent over 1,000,000 *livres* in Palestine after his disastrous campaign in Egypt was over. Quite early on it became clear that sources of finance other than crusaders' pockets would have to be tapped.

Rulers soon came to demand subsidies from their subjects. In 1146 Louis VII imposed on France a general census to raise money for the Second Crusade: it is not clear what form this took, but it was charged on the Church as well as the laity and may have been a forced feudal levy. In 1166 a tax for the Holy Land, based on the value of movable property and income, was collected by Louis and Henry II of England. In 1185 Henry of England and Philip of France levied a graduated tax on income and movables and demanded a tenth of the alms left by those who died in the ten years following 24 June 1184. In 1188 Henry imposed the famous Saladin Tithe for one year on the income and movables of those, clerks and laymen, who did not take the Cross, and in June 1201 the papal legate Octavian persuaded John of England and Philip of France to contribute a fortieth of a year's income from their lands and to raise the same from the estates of their vassals. These occasional taxes are to be found throughout the thirteenth century: for instance Louis IX of France pressed towns to give him money for his crusade in the 1240s and in 1270 the English parliament granted the Lord Edward a crusade twentieth. In 1274 Pope Gregory X demanded, with what success is not known, that every temporal ruler levy from each subject one silver penny.

The value of the alms and legacies of the faithful, given from the first and particularly in the outburst of popular enthusiasm which had followed the conquest of Palestine, was appreciated by the popes, who ordered that chests be placed in churches for their collection, from the middle of the twelfth century granted Indulgences, though not plenary Indulgences, to those who contributed to the movement in this way, and encouraged the faithful to make bequests to the Holy Land in their wills.

The popes themselves naturally played the most important part in the financing of crusades. They exploited the normal judicial processes of the Church – under Gregory IX and Gregory X the proceeds of fines imposed on blasphemers were sent to the Holy Land – but they also took new measures. They began to allow the redemption of crusade vows for money payments. Several different trains of thought led to this important development. First, the belief that all should contribute in some way to the movement was reflected in the growing practice of granting Indulgences in return for donations rather than participation. Secondly, the Church was faced by large numbers who were in fact incapable of fighting but had taken the Cross, in spite of the general feeling that they should not participate in the crusades. One of the reports of Urban's sermon at Clermont made him state that no old men or women without husbands or suitable companions or priests without licence should take part, and in his letters to Bologna and Vallombrosa he forbade some religious to go under any circumstances, other clerks without permission, young married men without the consent of their wives and parishioners without first seeking advice. In 1188 Henry II of England laid down that most of his crusaders were not to take women and at about the same time the writer Ralph Niger inveighed against those clerics, monks, women, paupers and old men who went on crusades. In 1208 Innocent III wrote to the faithful in Lombardy and the March, proposing that those who were not capable of fighting should send soldiers in their place at their own expense. Thirdly, churchmen and canon lawyers had to deal with those who had taken the Cross in the first flush of enthusiasm and then wanted to be dispensed from their vows. As early as the tenth century it had been considered possible to send someone in one's place on pilgrimage and in the twelfth century, while it was difficult to get relaxation from the obligations of a crusade vow, it was not impossible – indeed it seems to have become quite common by the time of the Third Crusade.

From the pontificate of Alexander III onwards popes in decretals and canon lawyers in their commentaries began to consider dispensation, substitution (the sending of another in place of the crusader), redemption (dispensation in return for a money payment) and commutation (the performance of another penitential act in place of the one originally vowed). In the early years of his pontificate Innocent III laid down some general rules. These were exceptionally severe in that they confirmed the Roman law concept of the hereditability of vows – a son must perform a vow undertaken and not fulfilled by his father – but they also stated that the pope, though only he, could grant delay in the performance of a crusade vow or its commutation or redemption; the amount to be paid in redemption should equal the sum that would have been spent had the crusader actually gone with the expedition. The influence of these rulings can be seen working from 1213 onwards in papal letters and the conciliar decree concerning the preaching of the Fifth Crusade, which referred to commutation, redemption and deferment, and in the actions of Robert of Courçon and Archbishop Simon of Tyre, the papal legates in France, who encouraged everyone, whatever his health and state, to take the Cross, causing great scandal but clearly in order that moneys could be raised from the subsequent redemptions. From 1240 onwards, in spite of papal admonitions, redemptions were being granted almost as a matter of course to anyone who asked for them or paid for them, although for a short period, following the loss of Palestine in 1291, they became much harder to obtain. Finance from them became very important as the thirteenth century progressed, but the system was open to great abuse and came in for much criticism – and it was only made worse by the half-hearted attempts of some popes to reform it.

The greatest financial contribution came from the direct taxation of the Church by the popes: a substantial part of Louis IX's expenses must have been paid for by the French clergy. The first hint of new ideas on the contribution of the Church to the crusades is to be found in letters of 1188 from Pope Clement III to the clergy of Canterbury and Genoa encouraging them to direct some of their wealth to the support of the crusade. Ten years later Innocent III ordered the prelates of Christendom to send men and money to the Fourth Crusade and he repeated this injunction in *Quia major* of 1213, but meanwhile, in December 1199, he had taken a momentous step. He had come to the conclusion that there was nothing for it but to impose a tax upon the whole Church, although, obviously worried about the possible reaction from the bishops, he assured them that this was not to become custom or law or establish a precedent and he informed them that he himself would send a tenth of his revenues to the aid of the East. He ordered the clergy to pay a fortieth of all their revenues, after deducting anything owed in unavoidable usurious contracts; a very few religious were allowed to pay a fiftieth. Provincial councils were to discuss the matter and within three months a council in each diocese was to organise collection with the aid of a Templar and a Hospitaller. With the advice of the same two brothers and leading local figures each prelate was to hire soldiers and provide poor crusaders with subsidies. The levy proved to be extremely difficult to raise: by 1201 it had been gathered neither in England nor in France and in 1208 it had not been collected even in parts of Italy. Although in 1209 Innocent III laid a tax on the churches in the domains of the crusaders against the Albigensians, it must have been the failure of the measure of 1199 that persuaded him not to ask for another levy in 1213. But two years later a twentieth for three years was demanded of the Church by the Fourth Lateran Council, although again emphasis was placed on the pope's own contribution. From this time onwards income taxes were built up into a regular system of taxation, the most extensive of them being promulgated in 1274 at the Second Council of Lyons, a sexennial tenth from which none was to be exempt. Usually apportioned at a tenth, these taxes were demanded of the universal Church or of the clergy in a single country for periods varying from one to six years. Settlement was normally sought in two equal instalments each year, although resistance was common and the payments were nearly always in arrears. At first the proceeds were paid to local crusaders or sent directly to the Holy Land, while the popes simply received accounts, but in 1220 Pope Honorius III was already overseeing the transmission of the moneys. By the middle of the thirteenth century it had become customary for the popes to grant the yield of the taxes to kings or lords who had promised to go on crusade; if the king did not then depart, the money, which had been deposited for him in monasteries, was delivered to papal merchants for sending to Rome. But such was the resistance of the temporal authorities to this practice that the popes seldom received all they should.

Enormous sums were raised from alms, bequests, redemptions and taxes and there was a need for some efficient machinery for their collection. In 1188 Pope Clement III had ordered bishops to appoint clerks to collect money and spend it on troops, but in 1198 Innocent III himself chose collectors from among the churchmen in each province; it was typical of his methods that although these were local men they were instituted directly by him. In the following year he left the organisation of his new tax on the clergy to the bishops, perhaps to assuage local feelings, but the lack of co-operation very soon led to officials being sent from Rome to oversee collection and Innocent returned to central control in 1213: his preachers in the provinces were also to be involved in the raising of money. Papal commissioners were put in charge of the new twentieth levied on the Church in 1215 and the whole system was carried further by Innocent's successor Honorius III. Papal collectors are to be found operating throughout the thirteenth century; and in 1274 all Christendom was divided into twenty-six districts administered by collectors and sub-collectors. The taxes of 1199 and 1215 were assessed by the clergy themselves, but in 1228 Pope Gregory IX ordered the papal collectors to choose for this task special deputies who were to compel local churchmen under oath to value clerical incomes in a district.

Preaching and finance were two fields in which the popes could make use of the highly developed bureaucracy of the Church and we can trace the emergence of a characteristically elaborate machinery to act on their behalf. But their problems did not end with the recruitment of crusaders and the raising of money to subsidise them. Where was a crusade to go? And how was it to be controlled on the way?

Strategy

Crusading strategy was a moral matter, for the Holy War, being also Just, had to be fought in a way that would achieve its ends most painlessly. Of course in the conditions of the time and given the impossibility of co-ordinating the movements of contingents from different parts of Europe so that they would all come to the same place on the same date, long-term planning could present crusaders with nothing more than some general guide-lines. Events would always overtake plans made in the West and the final decisions had to be left to councils-of-war held on the spot. In 1238 the Christian leaders in Palestine suggested to Thibaut of Champagne that the fleet bringing his crusade ought to apply to Limassol in Cyprus, where it could refit and revictual. Here a council-of-war would discuss whether it was best to proceed to Syria or to Egypt; Limassol, they pointed out, was equally distant from Acre, Alexandria and Damietta. Although in the 1240s King Louis IX of France had clearly made plans to invade Egypt from the start, he did not give the final orders until his arrival in Cyprus. Some general planning, however, was made in the West. Pope Innocent III began the practice of receiving frequent reports from local Christians on political conditions in the East – he certainly took advice from them when making plans for the Fifth Crusade – and from the 1270s onwards there survive many memoirs written for the popes, most of which were composed in the early fourteenth century when the Christians had lost the Holy Land and a major effort was needed to recover it. Perhaps the most revealing insight into discussions on strategy can be found in King James I of Aragon's description of a debate at the Second Council of Lyons in 1274 in which both he and Pope Gregory X took part. Present were leaders of the Military Orders and experienced crusaders, among whom there seems to have been general agreement that large, elaborately organised crusades were expensive, often difficult to provision and support and did little long-term good. In fact a new strategic approach had been dominant since the 1250s, with an emphasis on the build-up of permanent garrisons in the Holy Land and the encouragement of small, manageable expeditions which could periodically succeed one another in the East. This was to remain the chief strategic thinking until the loss of all the Palestinian mainland in 1291. One often reads of a decline in crusading fervour after the middle of the thirteenth century, but this can be exaggerated: historians have been misled by the disenchantment with large international expeditions and the change in strategy in favour of small locally organised crusades.

Control

The crusades were papal instruments, the most spectacular expressions of the Papal Monarchy, the armies of the Christian Republic marching in response to calls from the men who on earth represented its monarch. We have seen that popes faced great difficulties in promoting and financing them and indeed the organisation needed was almost beyond the abilities of men of the time. But once an army had been collected together, the logistic problems solved and a goal set, the troops had to be controlled at a distance and this was the most difficult task of all. From the First Crusade onwards popes were represented in the armies by legates. A legate would be appointed to supervise the whole crusading army, but there could also be subordinate legates chosen to oversee national or regional contingents, though their relationship with their superiors was not always easy: on the Second Crusade Arnulf of Lisieux and Godfrey of Langres, each assisted by a man from his diocese, were papal representatives with the Anglo-Norman and French crusaders, but did not get on happily with Theodwin and Guy, the legates to the whole expedition. Legates were always churchmen and herein lay an insuperable problem. The popes and their representatives were priests and as such were forbidden by canon law to take up arms and fight. Conduct and temporal direction of the crusades, therefore, could not belong to them. This was expressed particularly clearly in c. 1150 by St Bernard, who wrote to Pope Eugenius III after being approached to lead a new crusade. How could he command military forces? It was now time, he wrote, to draw the two swords, spiritual and temporal, at the pope's disposal. Both St Peter's swords must be drawn, one by his hand, but the other at his command, for it seems that Peter himself was not personally to wield the temporal weapon, as he had been ordered by Christ on the eve of the crucifixion to put up his sword into his scabbard.

One legate whose powers have been studied closely is Adhemar of Le Puy, appointed 'leader' of the First Crusade. The general conclusion seems to be that, to Pope Urban, Adhémar's leadership was to be understood not as captaincy but in the context of spiritual duties, expressed through advice, arbitration and exhortation. The limitations on

Adhémar's powers of command are paralleled over and over again in the history of the crusades, and it is not surprising that the Fourth Lateran Council was irritatingly vague on the responsibilities of priests in the Christian army, who

> should diligently devote themselves to prayers and exhortations, teaching the crusaders both by word and example, so that they may always have before their eyes Divine Fear and Love and do not say or do anything that offends the Divine Majesty.

Pope Innocent III wrote with regard to another legate: 'As Joshua fights he ascends with Aaron the Mount of Contemplation and prays.' An exception, it has been suggested, was Pelagius of Albano on the Fifth Crusade and certainly Pelagius's very active role on campaign was criticised at the time. But the papal letter that set out his duties was perfectly in accord with tradition and at no time was his military leadership officially sanctioned: it was rather that on an expedition with no universally accepted captain Pelagius, who had great strength of personality, was able to dominate the councils-of-war. He did not command: he advised and tried to get general consent to his proposals; and his advice was not always taken.

Canon law, in fact, made the pope and his legate dependent on the goodwill of secular leaders, who alone could exercise military command. Over the most potent expression of his temporal claims a pope had very little control once an army was on the move and he could only watch helplessly if it was carried off course. This point has not been stressed enough with regard to the most tragic travesty of all, the assault by the Fourth Crusade upon the Byzantine Empire. There has been much debate on this diversion and all sorts of theories have been put forward to explain it. The least acceptable is that which makes Innocent III a party to a plot in the West to divert the crusade to Constantinople, for it credits the pope with far more power than he actually possessed. One must not confuse what he did after the expedition was over with his attitude before and during it. There is no doubt that a very short time after the capture of Constantinople he was engaged in an all-out effort to subordinate the Greek Church to Rome. In his demands for conformity he was doing something new – such a rigorous attitude towards the eastern Churches was not hitherto to be found in the Latin states in the East – but his acceptance and exploitation of a novel situation, however unattractive this might appear to be to us, should not be taken as evidence that from the start he was involved in plans to conquer Greece. We have seen that he was obsessed by the crusades and by the need to help the Holy Land. In the years 1202 to 1204 he was also comparatively young and inexperienced. Faced by a group of ruthless politicians, who actually prevented the legate Peter Capuano from joining the crusade at Venice, and by a leviathan that went lumbering away out of control, his compliance and long silences, which have aroused suspicion, can surely best be interpreted as hesitation, an inability to decide how to put his precious instrument back on its right path.

We have seen that the authority which legitimised this form of the Holy War was the papacy; that the crusaders' vows enabled a temporal activity to be brought under some ecclesiastical authority; that the popes could act with effect in the proclamation, preaching and financing of a crusade; but that once the army was on the march their powers were more theoretical than real. No spiritual leader, however exalted, could really exercise control over so secular an affair as war.

4 *Who Were the Crusaders?*

The Vow

THERE could be no crusade without crusaders and what made a man a crusader was the taking of a vow. This vow was introduced by Pope Urban II when at Clermont he asked his audience to make promises and told those who answered his call to sew crosses on their clothes as a public sign of their commitment. This was a new element in the Christian Holy War, although it was the product of a train of thought already in his mind before November 1095: at Piacenza in the previous March he had replied to the appeal from the Greeks by urging men to take an oath to help God and the Byzantine emperor against the pagans. Of course Christian vows had had a long history and for a long time had been viewed as creating legally binding obligations, but over the next century and a half they were to be treated exhaustively by canon lawyers. They came to be defined as deliberate commitments made to God to do or not to do certain acts. They could be simple, made with no formalities and therefore not enforceable as far as the Church was concerned, or solemn, publicly taken, expressed in the present tense and legally binding; general, obligatory on all Christians, or special, resulting in individual, voluntary acts; necessary, in that they were needed for salvation, or voluntary, undertaken out of personal devotion; pure, being absolute commitments, or conditional. A man would go through several stages — termed *deliberatio, propositum* and *votum* — before he was definitely committed, but once he had taken a *votum* this, if unfulfilled, was binding on his heirs, although in certain circumstances he could be dispensed from it or could commute it. The definition just given was the product of a long period of development, but it is a useful starting-point from which to describe the vow to crusade. This was usually solemn, always special and voluntary and often conditional. It resulted in a temporary commitment which in terms of the expeditions to the East seems generally to have been to visit the Holy Sepulchre in Jerusalem with the qualification that the pilgrimage must be made in the ranks of an organised armed expedition authorised by the pope. Surviving evidence for the Albigensian Crusade suggests that in that case the vow was made to war against the heretics and enemies of the faith in Languedoc. There was a very close relationship between the vows of crusaders and pilgrims. Canon lawyers made little differentiation between them and it was only around the year 1200 that they mentioned the crusaders' vows independently; the obligation of a crusader was to make what was regarded as a kind of pilgrimage and many of his privileges had previously been enjoyed by pilgrims; the rites for the taking of the Cross (of which, incidentally, none survives before the later twelfth century: they may not have developed independently before that time) appear to have been variants of those for making pilgrimages and it is probable that they derived from them: crusaders could even be invested with the scrip and staff of pilgrims as well as with the cross that marked their special promise.

Privileges

The taking of the vow and participation in a crusade had consequences for the status and rights of the man involved. He became, as we have seen, a kind of temporary ecclesiastic, subject to the courts of the Church. The vow he had made was a means by which his immediate enthusiasm could be turned into a legal obligation, enforceable by the judges to whom he was now answerable, and as early as the First Crusade the papacy was prepared to excommunicate those who failed to carry out what they had promised. The church courts would impose, or threaten to impose, the ecclesiastical sanctions of excommunication, interdict and suspension on reluctant crusaders, though canon lawyers went so far as to propose the disinheritance of heirs who did not carry out the unfulfilled vows of their dead fathers. But crusaders also gained the right to enjoy certain privileges as soon as they had taken the Cross or at least had begun to fulfil their obligations. It must be stressed that the Indulgence was not necessarily one of those that came into effect immediately, for it could not be decided whether it became effective on the taking of the vow or after the performance of the act for which the vow had been made. It will therefore be discussed separately.

The other privileges are often listed under the headings of spiritual rights, those contributing to the good of a crusader's soul, and temporal, those pertaining to his physical well-being. But all of them, apart from the right to benefit from the prayers offered for crusaders by the universal Church, which was not technically a privilege at all, were in fact legal exemptions from the operation of the courts or invitations to the courts to act on the crusader's behalf. They are perhaps better divided into those which eased the life of a crusader in a world of legal niceties and technicalities and those which were descended from or were elaborations of the original privileges enjoyed by pilgrims.

The first group can be quickly dealt with. One of them, the licence to clerics who joined the crusade to enjoy their benefices for a time, even though non-resident, and to pledge them to raise money for the journey, is to be found in the twelfth century, although it was not fully confirmed by the papacy until the thirteenth. The rest were granted from the pontificate of Innocent III onwards and by the middle of the thirteenth century may be summarised as: release from excommunication by virtue of taking the Cross; the licence to have dealings with excommunicates while on crusade without incurring censure; the right not to be cited for legal proceedings outside one's native diocese; freedom from the consequences of an interdict; the privilege of having a personal confessor, who was often allowed to dispense his patron from irregularities and to grant pardon for sins, like homicide, which were usually reserved for papal jurisdiction; and the right to count a crusade vow as an adequate substitute for another vow made previously but not yet carried out.

The privileges of the second group are more important. At the time of the First Crusade pilgrims were subject in the same way as clerics to church courts; their persons were protected from attack, a security that was reinforced as the Peace Movement gained ground; they were assured that lands and possessions seized by others during their absence would be returned to them; they could demand hospitality from the Church; they were in theory exempted from tolls and taxes and immune from arrest; and they may already have had the right to a suspension of legal proceedings in which they were involved until their return. Crusaders enjoyed the same rights from the first. As temporary churchmen they were subject in all but a few exceptional matters to ecclesiastical law and were exempt from secular jurisdiction in cases that arose after they had taken the Cross. At Clermont Urban II accorded them the protection of the Truce of God and throughout the papacy stressed that their persons should be secure. In their absence their families and properties were protected by the Church, which assumed this duty during or very soon after the First Crusade. Cases on the question were already being examined by ecclesiastical judges very early in the twelfth century and the principles were stated at the First Lateran Council and in *Quantum predecessores,* to be constantly repeated thereafter.

> And we decree that their wives and children, goods and possessions should remain under the protection of Holy Church; under our protection and that of the archbishops, bishops and other prelates of the Church of God. And by apostolic authority we forbid any legal suit to be brought thereafter concerning any of the possessions they held peacefully when they took the Cross until there is absolutely certain knowledge of their return or death.

> Since [wrote Pope Gregory VIII to the crusader Hinco of Serotin in 1187] you. . . having assumed the sign of the living Cross, propose to go to the aid of the Holy Land, we. . . take under the protection of St Peter and ourselves your person, with your dependants and those goods which you reasonably possess at present, . . . stating that they all should be kept undiminished and together from the time of your departure on pilgrimage overseas until your return or death is most certainly known.

The Church itself, through the agency of the bishops or, in the cases of some important crusaders, of special officials called *conservatores crucesignatorum,* oversaw the protection of the lands. It was common, particularly in England where the crown often acted as the guardian of their property, for crusaders also to appoint attorneys to defend their interests in their absence. Crusaders also came to be entitled to *essoin,* a delay in the performance of services and in judicial proceedings to which they were a party until their return; to a quick settlement of outstanding court cases if they so willed; to permission to count the crusade as restitution of some article stolen; to the right to dispose of or mortgage fiefs or other property which was ordinarily inalienable; to a moratorium on debts and exemption from interest payments while on crusade; and to a freedom from tolls and taxes.

Then, of course, there was the Indulgence. A question that much concerned canon lawyers in the thirteenth century was whether this was effective from the moment the Cross was taken or only once the crusade had been accomplished: in other words, was it consequent upon the making of the vow or the performance of the act for which the vow was made? This was important since upon a ruling hung the hopes of heavenly reward for crusaders who died before completely fulfilling their vows or even before they had begun to carry them out. St Thomas Aquinas was of the opinion that the wording of the papal grants of Indulgence was vital here: if an Indulgence had been conceded to those who took the Cross for the aid of the Holy Land, then the condition of the Indulgence was merely the making of the vow and not the journey; if, on the other hand, an Indulgence had been given specifically to those who went overseas, then the condition, the crusade itself, must be fulfilled before it could be effective. But it is clear that there was not universal agreement on the matter, which was complicated by the fact that Indulgences could also be granted to those who participated in crusades but took no vows at all. All one can be certain of is that, unlike other privileges, the Indulgence was not an automatic consequence of the taking of the vow.

But what was the Indulgence? Official teaching is that, after confession, absolution and the performance of the works that earn it, a sinner is granted by the Church on God's behalf remission of all or part of the penalties that are the inevitable consequence of sin. This remission applies not only to the canonical punishment imposed by the Church itself, usually by a priest in the confessional, but also to the temporal punishment imposed by God either in this world or in the next. The doctrine is influenced by the distinction between the guilt of and the punishment due for sin, known to Hugh of St Victor and Gratian in the early twelfth century, and by the concept, only fully formulated in the thirteenth century but present in an embryonic form much earlier, of the Treasury of Merits, an inexhaustible credit-balance of merit stored up by Christ and the saints on which the Church can draw on behalf of a repentant sinner. The first Indulgence is only to be found in the middle of the eleventh century, the theory of Indulgences developed with the crusades, and the early grants display a deplorable vagueness of purpose and confusion of terminology. It is, therefore, generally agreed that the Indulgence as we know it cannot have been fully accepted, at an official level, until the thirteenth century, although, whatever the popes and their advisers may have thought, ordinary Christians assumed from the first that it meant a remission of all punishment due for sin, an assurance of direct entry into heaven. It is, however, possible that the developed view of the Indulgence began to be accepted in Rome rather earlier than is nowadays supposed.

In 1063 what was arguably the first recognisable Indulgence was granted by Pope Alexander II to warriors in Spain: 'We, by the authority of the holy apostles Peter and Paul, both raise their penance from them and make remission of their sins.' It is clear that two ideas were present in this formulation. First, penance, the penalty enjoined by the Church, was waived, but secondly, sins were remitted. It was the expression *remissio peccatorum,* remission of sins, which came closest to the developed Indulgence, since it referred to the extinction of the sins involved, and therefore presumably of their consequences, without distinction between penance and divine punishment. Urban II used the term twice, in his letter to Flanders in 1095 and in 1098–9, when he granted to those defending Tarragona in Spain the same Indulgence as was given to crusaders, but he was not consistent, for he also drew upon the other strand of thought to be found in Alexander's letter. Canon 2 of the Council of Clermont declared:

> Whoever for devotion only, not for honour or financial gain, joins the expedition for the freeing of the Church of God in Jerusalem, can count that journey as a substitute for all penance.

Here we have simply the dispensation from the penance enjoined for a sin in return for the performance of another penitential act. The conciliar canons as they have come down to us are not entirely trustworthy, but in this matter they are echoed in Urban's letter to Bologna, in which, with a reference to Clermont, he assured those who went

> only for the salvation of their souls and the liberation of the Church, by the mercy of God and the prayers of the Catholic Church and by our authority and that of nearly all the archbishops and bishops in Gaul, we remit all penance for those sins for which they will have made true and perfect confession.

We may conclude that Urban himself had not fixed on a definite terminology for the Indulgence and was probably unclear in his own mind about it. The same was true of his successor, Paschal II, who in 1099 wrote of the remission of sins, but in 1101 of the remission of penance.

Uncertainty persisted during the next half-century, although there can be discerned a tendency towards the idea of the remission of sins rather than penance. There are statements on the remission or pardon of sins in the decrees of the First Lateran Council in 1123 and in an encyclical of Pope Adrian IV in 1157, and the idea was especially prominent in the preaching of the Second Crusade. St Bernard wrote of 'the Indulgence of sins and eternal glory' and told his correspondents:

> Receive the sign of the Cross and the supreme pontiff, the vicar of him to whom it was said, 'Whatever you loose on earth will be loosed in heaven', offers you that full Indulgence of all sins of which you have made confession with a contrite heart.

Pope Eugenius III's letter *Quantum predecessores* of 1145, in spite of looking back to the precedent set by Urban II, went quite a long way towards the developed view of the Indulgence, perhaps under St Bernard's influence.

> By the authority of omnipotent God and Blessed Peter the Prince of the Apostles, conceded to us by God, we grant remission of and absolution from sins, as instituted by our aforesaid predecessor, in such a way that whosoever devoutly begins and completes such a holy journey or dies on it will obtain absolution from all his sins concerning which he has made confession with a contrite and humble heart; and he will receive the fruit of everlasting recompense from the rewarder of all.

But the most important step was taken by Pope Alexander III. In 1165, when he published his first call to crusade, he simply issued a version of *Quantum predecessores,* including, of course, the reference to the Indulgence quoted above. And in *In quantis pressuris* of the following year he granted 'that remission of sins which Pope Urban of pious memory and our predecessor Eugenius instituted' and wrote of 'absolution from all sins', related to the merits of SS Peter and Paul, and 'remission of all sins'. The significance of these phrases becomes clearer when they are compared to a careful reference to the remission of enjoined penance elsewhere in the letter and we may conclude that to whoever drafted it the remission of sins was not meant to apply only to the penalties imposed in confession. This was rash and one can perhaps detect anxiety at the papal *Curia,* for by 1169, when the next crusade encyclical, *Inter omnia*, was published, there had been a change of heart. *Inter omnia* made reference to the remission of sins, but it also contained a remarkably cautious statement on the Indulgence, referring to it as 'that *remission of penance imposed by the priestly ministry* which Urban and Eugenius are known to have established'. There could be no doubt what kind of Indulgence was being granted here, for the term *remission of penance* was strengthened by the additional reference to the priest in the confessional and Alexander stressed this in a letter of the same day to the Archbishop of Rheims, in which he wrote of 'Indulgence of penances'. But over the next twelve years the papal *Curia* changed its mind again, and this time finally. This change may have taken place in the early 1170s, when there was, in a bull for the crusade against the Slavs, a reference to the remission of sins. But it had definitely occurred by 16 January 1181 when Alexander issued a new crusade encyclical, *Cor nostrum*. Parts of it were modelled on *Inter omnia*, so any differences are significant. In it, for those who fought for two years in the Holy Land

by the authority confided in us on behalf of the piety of Jesus Christ and the blessed apostles Peter and Paul we grant them absolution from all their crimes concerning which they have made confession with contrite and humble hearts.

This was, of course, far from being a really precise statement of the fully developed doctrine of Indulgences, but in comparison with the vacillation that had gone before its firmness is very striking and it is worth mentioning that thenceforward all papal letters, save one of Celestine III·which contained muddled drafting, referred to the remission of sins rather than of penance, adding, from Innocent III's pontificate when the formula reached its definitive form, the phrase 'and we promise them a greater share of eternal salvation as the reward of the just'. It is as if we can see the papal *Curia* making up its mind and deciding to follow the course that would lead, if it had not done so already, to the idea of the Indulgence as we know it. And by the early thirteenth century even the higher clergy had our idea of Indulgences, as we can see from one of James of Vitry's sermons.

Crusaders who, truly contrite and confessed, are girded in the service of God and then die in Christ's service are counted truly as martyrs, freed from both venial and mortal sins and from all enjoined penance, absolved from the penalties for sin in this world, from the penalties of purgatory in the next, secure from the torments of Gehenna, crowned with glory and honour in eternal beatitude . . . . Do not in any way doubt that this pilgrimage will not only earn you remission of sins and the reward of eternal life, but it will also offer much to wives, sons, parents, living or dead: whatever good you do in this life for them. This is the full and entire Indulgence which the supreme pontiff, according to the keys committed to him by God, concedes to you.

Who Were the Crusaders?

Two features of the vow were that it could be taken by anyone, of whatever sex or walk of life, and that the action promised was essentially temporary: a layman or a priest would put his normal occupation aside for a short time to go crusading. Historians of the crusades refer often to kings, magnates and knights and also describe the movements among the peasantry, but it is important to remember that the appeal of the crusades was confined to no class and a significant part was played by artisans, merchants, burgesses of all kinds, and even criminals whose sentences could be commuted in return for participation or settlement in the Holy Land. In the late twelfth century attempts were being made in England to list the crusaders living in certain areas: in Lincolnshire they were nearly all poor and included a clerk, a smith, a skinner, a potter, a butcher and a vintner; 43 crusaders were to be found in the archdeaconry of Cornwall, including a tailor, a smith, a shoemaker, 2 chaplains, a merchant, a miller, 2 tanners and 2 women. In 1250 the ship *St Victor*, bound from France to the East, was carrying 453 crusaders, of whom 14 were knights and leaders of groups, 90 retainers and 7 clerics; the remaining 342 passengers were commoners and the surnames of several of them suggest burgess origins; 42 were women, 15 of whom accompanied their husbands. 1 travelled with her father and 2 with their brothers.

Taking part in a crusade, therefore, would be men and women of all classes, even in the thirteenth century when redemption would have enabled many to have released themselves by making money payments. It would be interesting to know how these heterogeneous bands of people were organised, but the subject has never been studied and one can only make some tentative suggestions. When a king like Louis VII or Philip II or Richard I, or a very important magnate like Thibaut of Champagne or the Lord Edward, took part it was natural that he should be in unquestioned command, although if two kings were on the same expedition they would never allow themselves to be subject to one another: the French troops on the Third Crusade remained obstinately independent of Richard of England even after the departure of Philip of France. Secondly, a knight like Geoffrey of Sergines, about whom more below, would organise his own band of followers and then of course lead them on campaign. Thirdly, groups of crusaders, thrown together by circumstances or drawn from the same region, would elect their own leaders. Such captains might be appointed temporarily – immediately after the arrival in Egypt of the first contingent of the Fifth Crusade the crusaders chose someone to command them until the rest of the army arrived – but full-time leaders were also elected and this procedure must have been very common: the thirteenth-century translator of the History of William of Tyre assumed that it was what had happened on the First Crusade. It can be seen in operation during the planning for the Fourth Crusade when Boniface of Montferrat was chosen as leader and also during the Fifth, for when they gathered for departure the participants from the Rhineland and the Low Countries elected William of Holland as captain and George of Wied as second-in-command; once in Egypt the crusaders appear to have been divided into nations and the Germans seem to have chosen Adolph of Berg to command them; after his death in 1218 George of Wied was elected to succeed him. It was no doubt essential for a noble to be chosen for such an office. Fourthly, authorities in the West might pick officers to command the contingents from their districts: at the time of the Fifth Crusade Italian towns like Asti and perhaps Sienna may have chosen commanders before the departure of their forces. Fifthly, at the initiative of a local magnate or a high ecclesiastic or town burgesses in the West, citizens might organise themselves into a confraternity, a common form of religious association, though here committed to the defence of Christendom. As early as 1122 a confraternity in Spain was playing a part in the reconquest and another in Toulouse was established by the bishop to participate in the Albigensian Crusade. Confraternities from Spain, Pisa, Lombardy and Tuscany, England and Châteaudun in France maintained bands of crusaders in the East, and their importance is shown by the significant part their leaders played in politics of the Kingdom of Jerusalem.

Crusaders drawn from so many walks of life must naturally have had a great many reasons for taking the Cross. Of course not all of them were moved by high ideals and at one time it was fashionable to explain the appeal of the crusades, especially the First, almost entirely in economic terms. There was economic misery in parts of France in the later eleventh century and recent studies have shown how complex social developments in the knightly class contributed greatly to the response from certain areas. The desire for a new life in a new land or even a sense of duty to one's family, which one could help by removing oneself from the scene, found expression in the reconquests of Spain and Sicily and in the colonisation movement east of the Elbe. They may also be revealed in the Latin conquest of Palestine and later of Greece. There can also be little doubt that the chance of leaving the country for a time with the privilege of having their lands, including recent gains, protected in their absence and a delay in any court proceedings that might be pending appealed to many who were in political or legal difficulties and there is often to be found a correlation between political disturbance and the popularity of the Cross in a district. It has recently been shown how the response in the late 1260s to crusade appeals in England was linked to the consequences of the civil war of a few years earlier: many of those whose acquisitions or behaviour during the war would have been subject to court investigation went on crusade with the Lord Edward, thus putting off any decision on their gains or actions for a few years.

But too much can be made of mundane motives at the expense of ideals. Economic and social pressures may have conditioned some men psychologically to answer Urban II's call in 1095, but it is important not to confuse the colonising movement which grew up once Palestine and Syria had been conquered with reactions at the time of the departure of the First Crusade. It is far-fetched to suppose that those in search of land, already available in Spain and Germany, clearly saw colonial gain at the end of a march of thousands of miles with unknown dangers on the way. One often finds, moreover, that the response to the appeals was to some extent conditioned by the attitudes of the great men in particular neighbourhoods: if these chose to go, others would follow. But if the magnates had strong economic motives they were surely in favour of staying at home. The ideals of the crusades must genuinely have attracted many. Participation in them expressed the most profound feelings of popular spirituality, and there can be little doubt that their spell lasted a very long time. Ordinary men were deeply moved by the concept of the new knight and by the desire to serve

Christ by taking up his Cross, by defending the Church and by physically occupying and holding the land sanctified by his presence. And the idea that here at last was a fruitful field of action for the layman – one that he was especially qualified to undertake – had a powerful appeal in an age when the priesthood was privileged and of great prestige, and the life of the laity was regarded very much as second best to that of the religious. Crusade sermons dwelt on these themes, and one cannot believe that the preachers would have persisted with them had they made no impression on those they were addressing.

Geoffrey of Sergines

The crusades were at their most popular between 1187 and 1250 and thereafter enthusiasm began to wane in an atmosphere of growing cynicism and indifference. We must not, however, exaggerate the decline, for the call to crusade would continue to inspire men for centuries. It would not be out of place to spend a few pages on the career of one of the leading crusaders of the mid-thirteenth century, although he is now almost forgotten. Geoffrey of Sergines (c. 1205–69) came from a village north of Sens and not far from Paris. His family had close links with the Church: a brother was abbot of S. Jacques-de-Provins; Peter of Sergines, the Archbishop of Tyre who was captured by the Muslims at the Battle of Gaza in 1244, may have been a relative; and so may have been Margaret of Sergines who was abbess of Montivilliers.

Geoffrey is mentioned by chroniclers in connection with military engagements in Palestine in 1242 and 1244. The most likely date for his arrival in the East would be 1 September 1239, with an inglorious crusade under Count Thibaut of Champagne and Duke Hugh of Burgundy which contained a number of officials and servants of the French crown. He returned to France in 1244 and then in 1248 travelled East with King Louis, to whom he had been closely attached as early as 1236, when he was permitted by his previous liege-lord, Count Hugh of Blois, to become the king's liegeman, the most effective means of formalising a close relationship, since one was bound to one's liege-lord before all other men. An intimacy between the two men is confirmed in John of Joinville's account of Louis's crusade. John wrote of Geoffrey as of one who, like himself, was among the king's closest confidants. He was one of a select band of eight companions who stood guard over the king at Damietta and throughout the crusade he was to be found in the king's council and entrusted with important duties. On 5 April 1250, as the crusade retired in disorder from Mansurah, he alone stood by and protected the king: Louis was later to say that Geoffrey had defended him against the Egyptians as a good valet swats the flies around his lord. Louis set out for home in April 1254 but before going he arranged to leave behind Geoffrey, who was made Seneschal of Jerusalem and given command of a special contingent of 100 knights, with money to employ additional crossbowmen and sergeants. The granting of these two different posts needs some explanation. The seneschalcy was the most prestigious and demanding of the great offices of the crown of Jerusalem and Geoffrey was to hold it until his death. In the absence of the king or regent, and provided the ruler had not appointed a lieutenant to represent him, the seneschal presided over meetings of the High Court, the most important of the royal courts in which all liege-vassals of the crown had the right to sit and speak. He was, therefore, *ex officio* the second man in the judicial hierarchy. He also supervised the *secrete*, the royal financial office and treasury, which worked according to Muslim practice. With this post Geoffrey became a fief-holder of Jerusalem and ranked among the political leaders of the kingdom. His long period of office must have given him an unrivalled experience of the working of the courts and royal administration, but one should not automatically infer from this that he had administrative abilities, because with his appointment can perhaps be seen a change in the way seneschals were chosen. Two of his successors, Robert of Crésèques in 1269 and John of Grailly from 1272 to 1278, were, like him, crusaders in command of regiments supported by the French crown and it may be that the King of France had demanded the seneschalcy for his captains as part of the deal by which he financed a permanent garrison in the Holy Land.

In time Geoffrey came to be appointed to offices within the kingdom that carried even greater responsibilities. From 1259 to September 1261 and from 1264 to 1267 he governed Palestine on behalf of absent regents and from September 1261 to 1263 and perhaps for a few months in 1264 he was regent himself. With only a few breaks, therefore, he ruled the Kingdom of Jerusalem from 1259 to 1267 and he did so well: alone of the governors of the period his reputation for severe though impartial justice was recognised by the chroniclers. 'He held the land well and the country at peace', wrote one, 'and he was a good justiciar'. Another wrote that he was a very strong justiciar and in his time hanged many thieves and murderers, nor was he willing to spare anyone because of his birth or the gifts he could give, nor on account of friendship or any other matter.

A particularly scandalous case resolved by him concerned a knight who had killed a Cypriot bishop and had taken refuge with the Pisans in Acre, the chief city of the kingdom. Geoffrey invaded the Pisan quarter with men-at-arms – a sign of a strong ruler was his attitude towards the powerful and highly privileged Italian merchants – and forced the Pisans to surrender the murderer to him.

In 1254 King Louis had also made Geoffrey captain of a French contingent left behind in the Holy Land and it was Geoffrey's activities as a military leader that brought him fame in the West. With his establishment of this force the King of France began a practice that he and his successors were to follow for several decades. Under captains like Geoffrey, Oliver of Termes, Erard of Valéry and Robert of Créseques, this company was one of the most formidable fighting forces in the Holy Land. Geoffrey, who also led his own private regiment in the 1260s, remained in over-all command of the French troops until his death. These were supposed to be financed by the French crown, but a rather ironical remark by the poet Rutebeuf suggests that they were already short of cash in the mid-1250s. In October 1265 the Patriarch of Jerusalem, the Masters of the Temple and the Hospital, Geoffrey and Oliver of Termes wrote to Louis on behalf of some merchants from whom they had borrowed 1500 *livres*. The merchants could not recover the money from the king because in a shipwreck on the way home they had lost the receipts with which they had been issued. Geoffrey and Oliver added that on Louis's authority they had borrowed another 2500 *livres* of Tours. In 1267 the patriarch wrote a long letter to the Commander of the Templars in France, with detailed instructions on the various diplomatic moves he was to make to help the cause of the Holy Land in the courts of western Europe. He pointed out that Geoffrey needed 10,000 *livres* of Tours a year to keep his forces, presumably both his own and those of France, in being: this may have been because in a military disaster the year before his troops had been badly knocked about. Some of his knights, the patriarch reported, were wanting to leave and so to pay them the patriarch himself and the Masters of the Temple and the Hospital had asked for 3000 *livres* of Tours from the crusade hundredth that was being levied on the French Church. But already in 1266 Louis had sent letters of credit to Geoffrey and to Erard of Valéry 'to retain knight pilgrims in the Holy land' and in June 1267 Geoffrey and Erard were issuing receipts and having the letters certified in Acre by the patriarch and the Masters.

Geoffrey returned briefly to the West in the early 1260s. At this time he took the Cross once more and planned to travel East with a large company of knights. On 13 February 1262 Pope Urban IV gave him licence, as a crusader, to have a portable altar at which Mass could be celebrated; his chaplain was permitted to administer the sacraments to his knights and companions; and he was exempted from any decree of excommunication or interdict issued by a papal agent or, interestingly, by the Bishop of Acre, unless his name was specifically mentioned in a papal decree. The next few years revealed his devotion to the crusading cause, which was to keep him in the East until his death and nearly bankrupted him. He was now commanding his own company as well as the troops paid for by Louis and in February 1263 Urban IV asked the King of France and the King of Navarre, who as Count of Champagne was a French landowner, to send the proceeds of a market tax, called the *denarius Dei* and normally used for charitable purposes, to Geoffrey himself, who had taken on his shoulders practically the whole weight of the guard of Palestine and whose livelihood was threatened by the burden: the pope granted Indulgences to those who paid the *denarius Dei* and those who administered it. Some time probably between February and June 1265 Urban's successor, Clement IV, was himself giving attention to Geoffrey's needs. In letters to Louis and to the Archbishop of Tyre, the collector of crusade taxes in France, he emphasised, as Urban had done, how completely Geoffrey had committed himself to the well-being of the Holy Land. But although aided financially by the French crown Geoffrey was now oppressed by poverty, was threatening to leave and had asked for a subsidy from the crusade hundredth in France. The pope had agreed to this and he wrote to Geoffrey, informing him that financial help was on its way and adding, by way of encouragement, that he recognised how much the Holy Land depended on him. 500 *livres* were paid over in June, but more was needed and in mid-1267 the patriarch reported that Geoffrey would have to leave Palestine to sell his fiefs in France unless cash arrived.

Geoffrey died on 11 April 1269. Although an active man and certainly not a failure as captain, seneschal, regent and lieutenant of regents, he was no intellectual: there is no evidence for this in the writings associated with the feudal nobility in Palestine, a society which was always ready to praise brain-power. And although he was brave and a good warrior we have evidence for one act of stupidity as a military commander. In August 1266 he was in command of an important part of the vanguard of a Christian army raiding into Galilee which was ambushed and badly mauled by Muslim troops because in the search for loot it had carelessly allowed too great a distance to separate it from the main body of Christians. Geoffrey's qualities were conventional – John of Joinville called him a 'good knight and prud'homme' – and they were summed up in a remarkable poem, *La complainte de Monseigneur Geoffrei de Sergines*, written in 1255–6 by the great French poet Rutebeuf, who knew the area of France from which Geoffrey came. To Rutebeuf Geoffrey was the finest of all knights, valiant and bounteous of soul. When he lived in France he was known as a gentle, courteous and debonair man with much love for God and Holy Church. He never deceived anyone, feeble or strong, and he was generous to poor neighbours.

> He loved his liege-lord so much
> That he went with him to avenge
> The shame of God over the seas.
> One ought to love such a prud'homme.
> With the king he moved and went,
> With the king he there remained,
> With the king he bore good and ill.
> There has never been such a man.

Geoffrey was severely honest and impartial as a judge. He was deeply loyal to St Louis, risking his life in defence of his king in the retreat from Mansurah in 1250. Earlier in the crusade, when hopes were still bright and the Christians were negotiating with the infidel the return of the city of Jerusalem in exchange for their conquests in Egypt, the Muslims had demanded Louis himself as a hostage. Geoffrey had fiercely opposed this in a council held in the Christian camp, saying that he would prefer them all to be killed or captured to the reproach of leaving their king a hostage with the enemy. He was very pious, which would explain why he got on so well with St Louis and also his devotion to the crusades. The popes of the 1260s wrote of him as one who was totally committed, to the extent of exercising a ministry: 'devoting himself wholly in the ministry for the Crucified One... the one and only minister in the defence of the Holy Land'. In fact he might be compared, though a layman, to a brother of one of the Military Orders and he must have had a strong influence on his son, who also took the Cross and fought with Charles of Anjou in southern Italy.

This devotion to the crusades must not be seen in isolation. Geoffrey was not the only man to identify himself with them. Careers like his were to be found not only in the Military Orders, but also among laymen like Erard of Valéry, John of Grailly and Oliver of Termes, whose remarkable life reveals almost as much commitment as does Geoffrey's. These free-lance crusaders, not necessarily attached to a major expedition, were heirs to a tradition of crusading that went back to the twelfth century. But in the 1250s and 1260s their kind of war against the infidel was coming to be accepted as the right one for the times, as there evolved the new strategy of the maintenance by western powers of permanent garrisons in the Holy Land, backed up by many small expeditions which could be put together quickly and would provide immediate aid. Geoffrey of Sergines, as a crusader, captain of the French forces in the East and commander of his own company, played a large part in the application of these ideas at a time when they were developing. His career shows how important a role one of these garrison captains could play in the affairs of the Holy Land and his commitment, paralleled in other lives, should make us think twice before suggesting that the crusading movement was losing momentum. An ideal that could inspire such men was still very much alive.

The Military Orders

It is questionable whether one ought to consider the brothers of the Military Orders at all in a chapter on crusaders. It is true that the Military Orders were founded as or developed into institutions closely associated with the crusading movement and inspired by its ideals, and it was because of this that some of them became very well-endowed. They were committed to the reconquest of Christian territory or to the defence of Christendom and they operated alongside the crusaders or in the same areas as they did. They were associated with the movement by its apologists, particularly St Bernard who, in his great defence of the Templars, the De laude novae militiae, developed with reference to them the theme of the new knighthood fighting on behalf of Christ. Some eight decades later James of Vitry defined their duties very much in terms of the crusades:

> The brothers of the Military Orders are ordained to defend Christ's Church with the material sword, especially against those who are outside it; that is against the Muslims in Syria, against the Moors in Spain, against the pagans in Prussia, Livonia and Comania... against schismatics in Greece and against heretics everywhere dispersed throughout the universal Church.

The Orders, he went on, differed in their habits and customs, 'but all are united in defence of the Church against infidels'. But however closely the Orders' aims were in accord with those of crusades, the brothers were not crusaders. Some, like the Templars, took vows which, at least in the actions to be performed, the reconquest of Jerusalem and the defence of the Holy Land, had similarities to those of crusaders, but others did not: the promises made by a brother of the Hospital of St John – to be obedient and chaste, to live in poverty as a serf and slave of the sick – made no reference whatever to the defence of Christendom. And even when a Military Order did impose a vow to defend Christendom upon its members, the form the promise took made it fundamentally different from that of a crusader. A brother of a Military Order was permanently committed to his duty; he was not a pilgrim, whose condition was essentially temporary, and so the concept of pilgrimage did not enter into his vow at all. This difference between the crusader and the brother of a Military Order was well brought out in one of James of Vitry's sermons, in which he told the story of a crusader who had been captured along with some Templars by the Muslims. On being asked if he was a Templar he replied, 'I am a secular knight and a pilgrim.'

It is not easy to generalise about the Military Orders because there were many of them and among them there was great variation. They followed different rules. Some, like the Orders of the Temple, the Hospital of St John and St Lazarus, drew recruits from all parts of Latin Christendom; others, like the Orders of St Mary of the Germans (the Order of the Teutonic Knights), Santiago, Alcantara, Calatrava and St Thomas, were nationally based. Some, like the Temple and the Hospital, were immensely rich; others were tiny and poor. Some were highly privileged, exempt from the authority of diocesan bishops and answerable only to Rome, prototypes of the great international Orders that grew up in the later Middle Ages – indeed the Orders of the Friars owed a great debt to the Templars and Hospitallers; others were in terms of privileges quite insignificant. The whole *raison d'être* of some was the defence of the faith; but others, like the Hospital of St John, had originated as purely charitable institutions which had only slowly, and then with the disapproval of the popes, turned themselves into Military Orders, and in them charitable activities remained their primary responsibility. Others still, like St Mary of the Germans, were founded both to fight and to care for the sick. But there were also some important and fundamental similarities. All were religious Orders, that is to say that they were religious institutes for which solemn vows were made and in which the brothers followed rules of life and the monastic *horarium* and submitted themselves to canonical discipline. Their essential characteristic was that a number of the professed lay brothers were themselves warriors. Any religious institution could have vassals owing military services or could employ mercenaries to garrison castles and protect territory, but these would not make it a Military Order. The Military Orders themselves made use of vassals and many mercenaries – in any engagement the number of brothers-at-arms in their forces was always comparatively small – but it was the class of fighting brothers that gave them their special features. And it was these lay brothers, rather than the priests as was normal in most religious Orders, who came to dominate them, being far more numerous and providing the great and lesser officers.

The Military Orders never had any difficulty in drawing in recruits, even as late as the eighteenth century, although their wealth, privileges and rivalries and a suspicion, very general in the West and rather unfair, that they were not pulling their weight made them increasingly unpopular with the clergy and with ordinary people in the thirteenth century. In fact their rules reflected the muscular qualities of the twelfth-century Latin Church; they showed none of the sympathy for alien ideas which after 1200 became a feature of the Christianity of St Thomas. Internationally run and highly privileged instruments of papal power, echoing contemporary notions of and ambitions for ecclesiastical organisation, the structures of the greater among them were if anything overelaborate and proved quite inadequate for their needs: organised on a vast scale, they were also massively incompetent. This led to the paradox that, although the spearheads of what were among the richest religious Orders of the time, the Convents in Palestine were always starved of money and often near bankruptcy.

The brothers in the East, standing to arms in a defensive war, marooned themselves in those magnificent fortresses which today still stand as mute monuments to the ideal of the just cause, the most beautiful and most depressing reminders of it. Yet by one of those quirks of history two of the Orders, the Hospitals of St John of Jerusalem and St Mary of the Germans, have survived. Both, especially the Hospital of St John on Rhodes until 1523 and on Malta until 1798, have played an important role into modern times and although today their tasks have greatly changed they are living relics of the age of the crusades.

5 *When Were the Crusades?*

WE ARE now coming to the end of our enquiry and have reached the stage at which we can made a definition. A crusade was a manifestation of the Christian Holy War, fought against the infidels in the East, in Spain and in Germany and against heretics, schismatics and Christian lay opponents of the Church for the recovery of property or in defence. Its cause was just in the traditional sense, but it was related to the needs of all Christendom or the Church, rather than to those of a particular nation or region, and it was because it was Christ's own enterprise that it was not merely justifiable but was positively holy. Legitimate authorisation was given to it by the pope as head of Christendom and representative of Christ, rather than by a temporal ruler. At least some of the participants took a vow which subordinated them to the Church and assured some papal control over them in matters other than the actual waging of war. A crusade was regarded as a form of pilgrimage and pilgrimage terminology was often used of the crusaders and their campaigns; the vow the crusaders took was based on that of pilgrims and so were many of the privileges they enjoyed in consequence of it, particularly the protection of themselves, their families and properties. They were also granted Indulgences and when they were not engaged in war in the East these were specifically related to those given to crusaders in the Holy Land.

One ought now to try to give chronological bounds to the movement. When was the first and when the last crusade? Some answer to the first of these questions can be found if we look before 1095 at one campaign, which has often been seen as a crusade, and at the plans for another. In 1063–4 a French expedition, led by the Duke of Aquitaine and associated with Catalans and Aragonese, took Barbastro in Spain. At the same time a Truce of God was proclaimed in Catalonia so that there should be peace behind the lines and Pope Alexander II issued the first Indulgence for the combatants. Here was an international army fighting the Muslims for the recovery of once Christian property, linked, as was the First Crusade, to a Truce of God and supported by the pope, who granted the participants an Indulgence. But there was no formal papal authorisation, no concept of pilgrimage and above all no vow made by those taking part and therefore no protection for them. It cannot be called a true crusade.

Following the Battle of Manzikert in 1071 the Seljuk Turks overran Asia Minor and the young Byzantine Emperor Michael VII, disregarding the bad feelings between the Latin and Greek Churches, appealed to the new Pope Gregory VII for aid. Gregory, hoping to bring the Churches together, reacted vigorously and there survive five letters written by him to various correspondents between February and December 1074. He dwelt on the sufferings of the eastern Christians and the necessity of bringing them fraternal aid. He compared service in the army to service of the Church, calling on one man 'to defend the Christian faith and the heavenly king', and he stressed the heavenly rewards that would result: in one letter he wrote that 'by momentous labour you can acquire eternal mercy' and in another he exclaimed that while it was glorious to die for one's fatherland it was still more glorious to die for Christ. The expedition was his own and he might lead it himself: he reported to King Henry IV of Germany that over 50,000 men were ready to go if they could have the pope 'in the expedition as leader and high priest' and he even suggested that under his leadership the army might push on to the Holy Sepulchre. He was thinking, extraordinarily enough, of leaving Henry behind to keep and defend the Roman Church in his absence. Much of this, of course, was hyperbole and the plans were given up when Gregory and Henry became involved in the Investiture Contest. But one can see here the concept of the Holy War and papal authorisation of it, some idea of eternal reward and also a reference to Jerusalem. Gregory's ideas may have been more developed than these letters reveal – he was later regarded as the father of the crusades – while what we know of Pope Urban II would make it very possible that he was merely following in the footsteps of his master. But on the evidence before us we cannot go so far. Gregory's letters contain no clear link between the planned expedition and pilgrimages, no Indulgence and, again, no sign of the vow and resulting protection for crusaders. Until further evidence comes to light one is forced to conclude that the plans of 1074 were not really those for a crusade, that the traditional date of 1095 for the origins of the movement is correct and that it stemmed from an initiative taken by Urban II.

It is still not possible to decide when the crusades came to an end. Certain elements long survived. Papal authorisations of war against Islam and grants of crusade Indulgences were made regularly up to the last quarter of the eighteenth century. The Knights of St John continued to wage an increasingly ineffective war against the Turks up to 1798, when they were driven from Malta by Napoleon, and their Order is still in existence. The *Bula de la cruzada*, giving rights based on those of crusaders, and the *cruzada*, an ecclesiastical tax linked to grants of Indulgences and minor privileges, were still to be found in Spain and Latin America into very modern times. But when was the last time that the essential elements of papal authorisation, the Indulgence and the vow, came together? The existence of papal letters proclaiming the crusade and granting Indulgences is not enough. When were the last crusaders? At the moment this question cannot be answered. There were certainly men who had taken the Cross in the sixteenth century and there may have been some in the seventeenth and even possibly in the early eighteenth century, fighting in the armies of Venice or Austria or the Holy League against the Turks. But the nearer we get to the present day the more the mists swirl in, obscuring our vision. Frankly, until some enterprising historian decides to research the subject and evidence of vows to crusade in this period comes to light, the last crusade, in the true sense of the term, cannot be dated. But we are left with the tantalising possibility that it took place less than three centuries ago.

Select Bibliography

This bibliography does not include translated sources. I feel strongly that the reading of scattered narrative accounts has little value for students, other than in showing them what medieval chronicles are like. And it can be positively misleading, for creative historical research does not rest on the uncertain foundations provided by a single witness, but involves the careful comparison of many fragments of evidence, coming in different forms and from different directions. It would be much more useful for the student if his instructor were to assemble as much translated evidence as possible for one incident or series of events; and this can be profitably done for each of the first four major crusades. Those who want to get hold of reasonable translations of many of the narrative accounts of the expeditions to the East will find references to them included in Mayer's *Bibliographie* (about which more below), and several of the local European chronicles and histories have also been translated.

H. E. Mayer, in his *Bibliographie zur Geschichte der Kreuzzüge* (Hanover, 1960), has compiled a first-class bibliography of books and articles published before 1958–9, containing over 5 000 titles. Professor Mayer issued a supplement for the years 1958–67 as 'Literaturbericht über die Geschichte der Kreuzzüge', in *Historische Zeitschrift, Sonderheft* 3 (1969), and his regular short reviews for *Deutsches Archiv für Erforschung des Mittelalters* are a good guide to what is being brought out year by year.

A competent and up-to-date short history of the crusades to the East is H. E. Mayer, *The Crusades* (Oxford, 1972). For the general reader the best of the large-scale works is S. Runciman, *A History of the Crusades*, 3 vols (Cambridge, 1951–4), which has the inner unity and interest which comes from the work of a single author, and for this reason is to be preferred to K. M. Setton (editor-in-chief), *A History of the Crusades*, 2nd. ed., 3 vols published so far (Madison, 1969–). This enterprise, often termed the 'Wisconsin History of the Crusades', suffers from the usual failings of collaborative projects and is far from being comprehensive, although some individual chapters are very good and others are on topics that are not easily read about elsewhere. J. Prawer, *Histoire du royaume latin de Jérusalem*, 2 vols (Paris, 1969–70) has some interesting things to say about the movement.

The crusades of the fourteenth century have been described by A. Z. Atiya, in *The Crusade in the Later Middle Ages* (London, 1938) and in vol. III of Setton (ed.), *A History of the Crusades* (referred to above), and briefly by A. T. Luttrell, 'The Crusade in the Fourteenth Century', in J. R. Hale *et al.* (eds), *Europe in the Late Middle Ages* (London, 1965). But this is a field in which a good, detailed work is badly needed; for the moment it is true to say that in many ways the best studies are two written in the nineteenth century: J. Delaville Le Roulx, *La France en Orient au XIVe siècle: Expéditions du maréchal Boucicaut*, 2 vols (Paris, 1885–6), and N. Iorga, *Philippe de Mézières (1327–1405) et la croisade au XIVe siècle* (Paris, 1896). Very little has been written on the crusades after 1400.

The historical background to and the development of the concept of the crusade were described in a great work by C. Erdmann, *Die Entstehung des Kreuzzugsgedankens* (Stuttgart, 1935), although his views were to some extent challenged in two important studies: M. Villey, *La croisade: Essai sur la formation d'une théorie juridique* (Paris, 1942), which is perhaps the best book yet written on the concept of the crusade; and P. Rousset, *Les origines et les caractères de la première croisade* (Neuchâtel, 1945). And·Erdmann's interpretation of Urban II's thinking at the time of the First Crusade has been questioned convincingly by H. E. J. Cowdrey, 'Pope Urban II's Preaching of the First Crusade', in *History*, LV (1970). Cowdrey has also summarised the attitude of the monastery of Cluny to the crusading movement: see his 'Cluny and the First Crusade', in *Revue Bénédictine*, LXXXIII (1973).

A contribution to our knowledge of the papal attitude towards war in the eleventh century has been made by S. Robinson, 'Gregory VII and the Soldiers of Christ', in *History*, LVIII (1973). The Just War itself has been studied by F. H. Russell, *The Just War in the Middle Ages* (Cambridge, 1975), and there is an interesting article by R. H. Schmandt, 'The Fourth Crusade and the Just-War Theory', in *Catholic Historical Review*, LXI (1975).

Canon law was the first concern of M. Villey in *La croisade* (referred to above), and he turned again to the subject in his 'L'idée de croisade chez les juristes du moyen âge', in *Relazioni del X congresso internazionale di scienze storiche*: III, *Storia del medio evo* (Florence, 1955). A significant contribution to the study of canon law is made by J. A. Brundage, *Medieval Canon Law and the Crusader* (Madison, 1969), and Brundage has also produced many interesting articles, among which might be mentioned:

'Cruce signari: The Rite for Taking the Cross in England', in *Traditio*, XXII (1966);

'A Note on the Attestation of Crusaders' Vows', in *Catholic Historical Review*, LII (1966);

'The Crusader's Wife: A Canonistic Quandary', in *Studia Gratiana*, XII (1967);

'The Crusader's Wife Revisited', in *Studia Gratiana*, XIV (1967);

'The Army of the First Crusade and the Crusade Vow: Some Reflections on A Recent Book', in *Medieval Studies*, XXXIII (1971).

In the last-mentioned study, Brundage shows beyond doubt that Urban II did introduce the vow in 1095.

The Indulgence has been discussed by J. A. Brundage, *Medieval Canon Law* (referred to above) pp. 145–55, by H. E. Mayer, *The Crusades* (referred to above) pp. 25–40, and by M. Purcell, *Papal Crusading Policy 1244–1291* (Leiden, 1975) pp. 35–98; but the most comprehensive work is N. Paulus, *Geschichte des Ablasses* (Paderborn, 1922–3). A. Gottlob's discussion in his *Kreuzablass und Almosenablass* (Stuttgart, 1906) is still useful.

The crusade was an instrument of the Papal Monarchy. Papal bulls from Urban II to Innocent IV are studied in U. Schwerin, *Die Aufrufe der Päpste zur Befreiung des Heiligen Landes von der Anfängen bis zum Ausgang Innozenz IV* (Berlin, 1937), and papal participation in the movement in the second half of the thirteenth century is examined in M. Purcell, *Papal Crusading Policy* (referred to above). An important work, establishing what happened at Clermont, is R. Somerville, 'The Councils of Urban II: Decreta Claromontensia', in *Annuarium Historiae Conciliorum*, Supplementum 1 (1972). Useful studies of the policies of Innocent III are H. Roscher, *Papst Innocenz III. und die Kreuzzüge* (Göttingen, 1969), and M. Maccarone, 'Studi su Innocenzo III. Orvieto e la predicazione della crociata', in *Italia sacra*, XVII (1972). For the financing of the crusades and developments in papal taxation, see especially W. E. Lunt, *Papal Revenues in the Middle Ages*, 2 vols (New York, 1934) and *Financial Relations of the Papacy with England*, 2 vols (Cambridge, Mass., 1939, 1962); and P. Guidi (ed.), 'Rationes decimarum Italiae nei secoli XIII e XIV. Tuscia. I. La Decima degli anni 1274–1280', in *Studi e Testi*, LVIII (1932).

Challenging contributions to the study of individual crusades to the East or of periods of crusading history are the following:

J. H. and L. L. Hill, *Raymond IV de Saint-Gilles, 1041(ou 1042)–1105* (Toulouse, 1959). These authors expounded their important view of the role of the legate Adhémar on the First Crusade in 'Contemporary Accounts and the Later Reputation of Adhémar, Bishop of Puy', in *Medievalia et Humanistica*, IX (1955);

G. Constable, 'The Second Crusade as seen by Contemporaries', in *Traditio*, IX (1953);

R. C. Smail, 'Latin Syria and the West, 1149–1187', in *Transactions of the Royal Historical Society*, 5th ser., XIX (1969);

G. B. Flahiff, 'Deus Non Vult. A Critic of the Third Crusade', in *Medieval Studies*, IX (1947);

J. P. Donovan, *Pelagius and the Fifth Crusade* (Philadelphia, 1950);

B. Z. Kedar, 'The Passenger List of a Crusader Ship, 1250: Towards the History of the Popular Element on the Seventh Crusade', in *Studi medievali*, 3rd ser., XIII (1972);

B. Beebe, 'The English Baronage and the Crusade of 1270', in *Bulletin of the Institute of Historical Research*, XLVIII (1975).

The best introduction to the views held of the crusades in the thirteenth century is in P. A. Throop, *Criticism of the Crusade. A Study of Public Opinion and Crusade Propaganda* (Amsterdam, 1940).

On Spanish crusades, a competent introduction is to be found in J. G. Gaztambide, *Historia de la Bula de la Cruzada en España* (Vitoria, 1958). See also C. J. Bishko, 'The Spanish and Portuguese Reconquest', in Setton (ed.), *A History of the Crusades*, vol. III (referred to above) and two studies by R. I. Burns: *The Crusader Kingdom of Valencia*, 2 vols (Cambridge, Mass., 1967) and *Islam under the Crusaders* (Princeton, 1973).

On Baltic crusades, see the narrative account by E. N. Johnson, 'The German Crusade on the Baltic', in Setton (ed.), *A History of the Crusades*, vol. III. Some sensible things about them have been written by F. Benninghoven in his *Der Orden der Schwertbrüder* (Cologne, 1965).

On the Albigensian Crusade, the best treatment in English is in W. L. Wakefield, *Heresy, Crusade and Inquisition in Southern France, 1100–1250* (London, 1974). Among other works one would recommend J. Madaule, *The Albigensian Crusade* (London, 1967) and P. Bellperon, *La croisade contre les Albigeois* (Paris, 1942).

Crusades against the lay powers in the West were treated in H. Pissard, *La guerre sainte en pays chrétien* (Paris, 1912), but see also:

J. R. Strayer, 'The Political Crusades of the Thirteenth Century', in Setton (ed.), *A History of the Crusades*, vol. II;

E. Kennan, 'Innocent III and the First Political Crusade', in *Traditio*, XXVII (1971);

P. Toubert, 'Les déviations de la Croisade au milieu du XIIIe siècle: Alexandre IV contre Manfred', in *Le Moyen Age*, LXIX (1963).

Twelfth-century warfare is the subject of R. C. Smail's magisterial study, *Crusading Warfare (1097–1193)* (Cambridge, 1956).

The best general history of the Military Orders before 1312 is still H. Prutz, *Die geistlichen Ritterorden* (Berlin, 1908). For individual Orders, see:

J. S. C. Riley-Smith, *The Knights of St John in Jerusalem and Cyprus, c. 1050–1310* (London, 1967);

J. Delaville Le Roulx, *Les Hospitaliers à Rhodes jusqu'à la mort de Philibert de Naillac (1310–1420)* (Paris, 1913);

R. Cavaliero, *The Last of the Crusaders. The Knights of St John and Malta in the Eighteenth Century* (London, 1960);

M. L. Bulst-Thiele, 'Sacrae Domus Militiae Templi Hierosolymitani Magistri', in
  Abhandlungen der Akademie der Wissenschaften in Göttingen, LXXXVI (1974);
M. Melville, *La vie des Templiers* (Paris, 1951);
M. Tumler, *Der Deutsche Orden im Werden, Wachsen und Wirken bis 1400* (Vienna,
  1955);
K. Forstreuter, *Der Deutsche Orden am Mittelmeer* (Bonn, 1967);
M.-L. Favreau, *Studien zur Frühgeschichte des Deutschen Ordens* (Stuttgart, 1974);
F. Benninghoven, *Der Orden der Schwertbrüder* (Cologne, 1965);
D. W. Lomax, *La Orden de Santiago, 1170–1275* (Madrid, 1965);
J. F. O'Callaghan, *The Spanish Military Order of Calatrava and its Affiliates* (London,
  1975).

On the Latin confraternities in the East, see J. S. C. Riley-Smith, 'A Note on Confraternities in the Latin Kingdom of Jerusalem', in *Bulletin of the Institute of Historical
Research*, XLIV (1971).

On Islamic history, recent works of especial interest are: E. Sivan, *L'Islam et la
croisade* (Paris, 1968); C. Cahen, *Pre-Ottoman Turkey* (London, 1968); and D. Ayalon,
'Studies on the Structure of the Mamluk Army', in *Bulletin of the School of Oriental and
African Studies*, XV–XVI (1953–4). There have been some good biographies of sultans,
in particular N. Elisséeff, *Nūr-ad-Dīn*, 3 vols (Damascus, 1967), and H. L. Gottschalk,
Al-Malik al-Kamil von Egypten und seine Zeit (Wiesbaden, 1958). A recent biography of
Saladin is A. S. Ehrenkreutz, *Saladin* (New York, 1972), but the study in preparation
by M. C. Lyons and D. Jackson promises to become the standard life of the crusaders'
most famous opponent.

List of Original Sources

The following are original sources to which reference is made directly or indirectly in the text.

Abbreviations

A.O.L. *Archives de l'Orient latin*
M.G.H. *Monumenta Germaniae Historica*, ed. G. H. Pertz *et al.* (Hanover/Weimer/Berlin/Stuttgart/Cologne, 1826 ff.)
M.G.H.S. *M.G.H. Scriptores* (in Folio et Quarto) 32 vols (1826–1934)
P.L. *Patrologiae cursus completus. Series Latina*, publ. J. P. Migne, 217 vols and 4 vols of indexes (Paris, 1844–64)
R.H.C. arm. *Recueil des historiens des croisades. Documents arméniens*, 2 vols (Paris, 1869–1906)
R.H.C. Oc. *Recueil des historiens des croisades. Historiens occidentaux*, 5 vols (Paris, 1844–95)
R.H.G.F. *Recueil des historiens des Gaules et de la France*, ed. M. Bouquet *et al.*, 24 vols (Paris, 1737–1904)

Acta imperii selecta, ed. J. H. Böhmer (Innsbruck, 1870)
Acta Pontificum Romanorum inedita, ed. J. von Pflugk-Harttung (Stuttgart,1888)
Adrian IV, Pope, 'Epistolae', *R.H.G.F.*, XV
Alexander III, Pope, 'Opera Omnia', *P.L.*, CC
'Annales Colonienses maximi', *M.G.H.S.*, XVII
'Annales de Terre Sainte', ed. R. Röhricht and G. Raynaud, *A.O.L.*, II (1884)
Annales ecclesiastici, ed. C. Baronius, O. Raynaldus, A. Pagi and A. Theiner, 37 vols (Bar-le-Duc/Paris, 1864–82)
'Annales Stadenses', *M.G.H.S.*, XVI
Aquinas: *see* Thomas
Baudri of Dol, 'Historia Jerosolimitana', *R.H.C. Oc.*, IV
Bernard of Clairvaux, 'De laude novae militiae ad milites Templi liber', *Sancti Bernardi Opera*, ed. J. Leclerq, C. H. Talbot and H. M. Rochais (Rome, 1963) vol. III
—, 'Epistolae', *P.L.*, CLXXXII; note also the translation of St Bernard's letters by B. S. James (London, 1953)
Bernold, 'Chronicon', *M.G.H.S.*, V
Boniface VIII, Pope, *Registre*, ed. G. Digard, M. Faucon, A. Thomas and R. Fawtier, 4 vols (Paris, 1884–1939)
Calixtus II, Pope, *Bullaire*, ed. U. Robert, 2 vols (Paris, 1891)
Cartulaire général de l'ordre des Hospitaliers de St-Jean de Jérusalem (1100–1310), ed. J. Delaville Le Roulx, 4 vols (Paris, 1894–1906)

Chroniques des églises d'Anjou, ed. P. Marchegay and E. Mabille (Paris, 1869)

Clement IV, Pope, *Registre*, ed. E. Jordan (Paris, 1893–1945)

Codex diplomaticus et epistolaris Moraviae, ed. A. Boček *et al.*, 15 vols (Olmütz, 1836–1903)

'Continuation de Guillaume de Tyr de 1229 à 1261, dite du manuscrit de Rothelin', *R.H.C. Oc.*, II

Corpus Juris Canonici, ed. A. Friedberg, 2 vols (Leipzig, 1879–81)

Diplomatarium Norvegicum, ed. C. R. Unger *et al.*, still in progress (Christiana [Oslo], 1847–)

'Documents et mémoires servant de preuves à l'histoire de l'île de Chypre sous les Lusignans', ed. L. de Mas-Latrie, *Histoire de l'île de Chypre* (Paris, 1852–5) vols II and III

'Documents relatifs aux Plaisançais d'Orient', ed. A. G. Tononi, *A.O.L.*, II (1884)

'Emprunts de Saint Louis en Palestine et en Afrique', ed. G. Servois, *Bibliothèque de l'Ecole des Chartes*, 4th ser., IV (1858)

Epistolae Pontificum Romanorum ineditae, ed. S. Löwenfeld (Leipzig, 1885)

Epistolae saeculi XIII e regestis pontificum Romanorum selectae per G. H. Pertz, ed. C. Rodenberg, *M.G.H.*, 3 vols (Berlin, 1883–94)

Epistulae et chartae ad historiam primi belli sacri spectantes, ed. H. Hagenmeyer (Innsbruck, 1901)

'L'estoire de Eracles empereur et la conqueste de la Terre d'Outremer', *R.H.C. Oc.*, I-II

Eugenius III, Pope, 'Epistolae et Privilegia', *P.L.*, CLXXX

'Fragmentum Historiae ex veteri membrana de tributo Floriacensibus imposito', *R.H.G.F.*, XII

Fulcher of Chartres, *Historia Hierosolymitana*, ed. H. Hagenmeyer (Heidelberg, 1913)

Geoffrey of Villehardouin, *La conquête de Constantinople*, ed. E. Faral, 2 vols (Paris, 1961)

Gerald of Wales (Giraldus Cambrensis), *Opera*, ed. J. S. Brewer (Rolls Ser., 21) 8 vols (London, 1861–91)

Gervase of Canterbury, *The Historical Works*, ed. W. Stubbs (Rolls Ser., 73) 2 vols (London, 1879–80)

Gesta Francorum et aliorum Hierosolimitanorum, ed. R. Hill (London, 1962)

Gesta regis Henrici secundi et Ricardi primi, ed. W. Stubbs (Rolls Ser., 49) 2 vols (London, 1867)

'Les Gestes des Chiprois', *R.H.C. arm.*, II

Gregory VII, Pope, *Epistolae vagantes*, ed. H. E. J. Cowdrey (Oxford, 1972)

—, *Registrum*, ed. E. Caspar, *M.G.H.* (*Epistolae selectae*, 2) 2 vols (Berlin, 1920–3)

Gregory IX, Pope, *Registre*, ed. L. Auvray, 3 vols and tables (Paris, 1896–1955)

Gregory X, Pope, 'Constitutiones pro zelo fidei', ed. H. Finke, *Konzilienstudien zur Geschichte des 13 Jahrhunderts* (Münster, 1891) pp. 113–17

Guibert of Nogent, 'Historia quae dicitur Gesta Dei per Francos', *R.H.C. Oc.*, IV

Hamburgisches Urkundenbuch, ed. J. M. Lappenberg *et al.*, 4 vols so far (Hamburg, 1907–67)

Helmold of Bosau, 'Chronica Slavorum', *M.G.H.S.*, XXI

Henry of Livonia, 'Chronicon Lyvoniae', *M.G.H.S.*, XXIII

'Historia Compostellana', *España Sagrada*, ed. H. Flórez *et al.* (Madrid, 1765) vol. XX

Historical Manuscripts Commission, *Fifth Report* (London, 1876)

—, *Report on Manuscripts in Various Collections* (London, 1901) vol. I

Honorius III, Pope, *Regesta*, ed. P. Pressutti, 2 vols (Rome, 1888–95)

Hostiensis, *Summa Aurea* (Basel, 1573)

Humbert of Romans, 'Opus Tripartitum', ed. E. Brown, *Fasciculus rerum expetandarum et fugiendarum* (London, 1690) vol. II

Innocent III, Pope, 'Opera Omnia', *P.L.*, CCXIV-CCXVI

—, 'Quia major', ed. G. Tangl, *Studien zum Register Innocenz III* (Weimar, 1929) pp. 88–97

—, *Register*, ed. O. Hageneder and A. Haidacher (Graz, 1964) vol. I

Innocent IV, Pope, *Commentaria in Quinque Libros Decretalium* (Turin, 1581)

—, *Registre*, ed. E. Berger, 4 vols (Paris, 1884–1921)

James I, King of Aragon, *Chronica*, ed. M. Aguiló y Fuster (Barcelona, 1873)

James of Vitry, *Lettres*, ed. R. B. C. Huygens (Leiden, 1960)

—, 'Sermones vulgares', ed. J. B. Pitra, *Analecta novissima* (Paris, 1888) vol. II

John of Joinville, *Histoire de Saint Louis*, ed. N. de Wailly (Paris, 1874)

John of Salisbury, *Historia pontificalis*, ed. M. Chibnall (London, 1956)

Layettes du Trésor des Chartes, ed. A. Teulet *et al.*, 5 vols (Paris, 1863–1909)

Martin IV, Pope, *Registre*, ed. Ecole française de Rome (Paris, 1901–35)

'A New Eyewitness Account of the Fourth Lateran Council', ed. S. Kuttner and A. García y García, in *Traditio*, XX (1964)

Odo of Châteauroux, 'Epistola', ed. L. d'Achery, *Spicilegium* (Paris, 1723) vol. III, pp. 624–8

—, 'Sermones de tempore et sanctis' ed. J. B. Pitra, *Analecta novissima* (Paris, 1888) vol. II

Odo of Deuil, *De profectione Ludovici VII in Orientem*, ed. V. G. Berry (New York, 1948)

Oliver of Paderborn, *Schriften*, ed. H. Hoogeweg (Tübingen, 1894)

Orderic Vitalis, *Historia ecclesiastica*, ed. A. Le Prévost (Paris, 1855) vol. IV; new ed. by M. Chibnall in progress (Oxford, 1969–)

Otto of Freising, *Gesta Friderici I Imperatoris*, ed. B. von Simson, *M.G.H.S. in usum scholarum* (Hanover/Leipzig, 1912)

Papsturkunden für Templer und Johanniter, ed. R. Hiestand (Göttingen, 1972)

'Papsturkunden in Florenz', ed. W. Wiederhold, *Nachrichten von der Gesellschaft der Wissenschaften zu Göttingen*, Phil.-hist. Kl. (Göttingen, 1901)

Papsturkunden in Spanien. I. Katalonien, ed. P. Kehr (Berlin, 1926)

Peter the Venerable, *Letters*, ed. G. Constable, 2 vols (Cambridge, Mass., 1967)

Quinque compilationes antiquae, ed. A. Friedberg (Leipzig, 1882)

Quinti belli sacri scriptores minores, ed. R. Röhricht (Geneva, 1879)

Ralph of Diceto, *Opera historica*, ed. W. Stubbs (Rolls Ser., 68) 2 vols (London, 1876)

Ralph Niger, 'De re militari et triplici via peregrinationis Jerosolimitanae', part ed. G. B. Flahiff, 'Deus Non Vult. A Critic of the Third Crusade', in *Medieval Studies*, IX (1947)

'Rationes decimarum Italiae nei secoli XIII e XIV. Tuscia. I. La Decima degli anni 1274–1280', ed. P. Guidi, in *Studi e Testi*, LVIII (1932)

Regesta pontificum Romanorum, comp. A. Potthast, 2 vols (Berlin, 1874–5)

La Règle du Temple, ed. H. de Curzon (Paris, 1886)

Robert of Clari, *La conquête de Constantinople*, ed. P. Lauer (Paris, 1956)

Robert the Monk, 'Historia Iherosolimitana', *R.H.C. Oc.*, III

Roger of Howden, *Chronica*, ed. W. Stubbs (Rolls Ser., 51) 4 vols (London, 1868–71)

Rutebeuf, *Onze poèmes concernant la croisade*, ed. J. Bastin and E. Faral (Paris, 1946)

Sacrae antiquitatis monumenta historica, dogmatica, diplomatica, ed. C. L. Hugo, 2 vols (Estival, 1725–31)

Sacrorum conciliorum nova et amplissima collectio, ed. G. D. Mansi, 31 vols (Florence/Venice, 1759–98)

Suger of S. Denis, 'Epistolae', *R.H.G.F.*, XV

—, *Vie de Louis le Gros. Suivie de l'histoire du roi Louis VII*, ed. A. Molinier (Paris, 1887)

Testimonia minora de quinto bello sacro, ed. R. Röhricht (Geneva, 1882)

Thesaurus novus anecdotorum, ed. E. Martène and U. Durand, 5 vols (Paris, 1717)

Thomas Aquinas, *Opera Omnia*, 25 vols (Parma, 1852–73)

Urban IV, Pope, *Registre*, ed. J. Guiraud, 4 vols (Paris, 1901–58)

Vetera monumenta historica Hungariam sacram illustrantia, ed. A. Theiner, 2 vols (Rome, 1859–60)

William of Malmesbury, *De gestis regum Anglorum libri quinque*, ed. W. Stubbs (Rolls Ser., 90) 2 vols (London, 1887–9)

William of Tyre, 'Historia rerum in partibus transmarinis gestarum', *R.H.C. Oc.*, I

Index

Index

The following abbreviations are used:

A   Abbot (of)   E   Emperor

Archbp Archbishop (of)   K   King (of)

B   Bishop (of)   p. leg. Papal Legate

C   Count (of)